Top Tips
from the
Baby Whisperer

Top Tips from the Baby Whisperer

Secrets to Calm, Connect and Communicate with your Baby

Tracy Hogg
with Melinda Blau

Vermilion
LONDON

7 9 10 8 6

Published in 2008 by Vermilion, an imprint of Ebury Publishing

Ebury Publishing is a Random House Group company

Copyright © Tracy Hogg Enterprises, Inc. 2001

Tracy Hogg has asserted her right to be identified as the author of this
Work in accordance with the Copyright, Designs and Patents Act 1988.

The Random House Group Limited Reg. No. 954009

Addresses for companies within the Random House Group can be found at

www.randomhouse.co.uk

A CIP catalogue record for this book is available from the British Library

The Random House Group Limited supports The Forest Stewardship
Council (FSC®), the leading international forest certification organisation.
Our books carrying the FSC label are printed on FSC® certified paper.
FSC is the only forest certification scheme endorsed by the leading
environmental organisations, including Greenpeace. Our
paper procurement policy can be found at
www.randomhouse.co.uk/environment

Printed and bound in Great Britain by Clays Ltd, St Ives PLC

ISBN 9780091917449

Copies are available at special rates for bulk orders.
Contact the sales development team on 020 7840 8487 or visit
www.booksforpromotions.co.uk for more information.

To buy books by your favourite authors and register for offers,
www.randomhouse.co.uk

The information given in this book should not be treated as a substitute for qualified medical advice;
always consult a medical practitioner. Neither the authors nor the publisher can be held responsible
for any loss or claim arising out of the use, or misuse, of the suggestions made or the failure to take
medical advice.

The anecdotes included in this book are not necessarily based upon the experiences of individuals.
A few of the portraits are composites, and in all cases names and identifying characteristics have been
changed to protect the privacy of individuals.

Contents

Introduction

Becoming the Baby Whisperer

Let me tell you straight away: I didn't dub myself 'the baby whisperer'. One of my clients did. But I kind of like it, because it does describe what I do.

Perhaps you already know what a 'horse whisperer' does, or possibly you've read the book or seen the movie of the same name. If so, you might remember how Robert Redford's character dealt with the wounded horse, advancing towards it slowly and patiently, listening and observing, but respectfully keeping his distance as he pondered the poor beast's problem. Taking his time, he finally approached the horse, looked it straight in the eye, and talked softly. The entire time, the horse whisperer stayed as steady as a rock and maintained his own sense of serenity, which, in turn, encouraged the horse to calm down.

Don't get me wrong, I'm not comparing newborns to horses (although both are sensate animals), but it's pretty much the same with me and babies. Parents think I have some special gift, but there's really nothing mysterious about what I do, nor is it a talent that only certain people possess. Baby whispering is a matter of respecting,

listening, observing and interpreting. You can't learn it overnight –
I've watched and whispered to over 5,000 thousand babies. But any
parent can learn; every parent *should* learn. I understand infants'
language, and I can teach you the skills you'll need to master it, too.

CHAPTER ONE
The Arrival of Your Newborn

The first three to five days are often the most difficult because everything is new and daunting. The first thing I tell parents – and keep telling them – is to sloooooooow down. It takes time to get to know your baby. It takes patience and a calm environment. It takes strength and stamina. It takes respect and kindness. It takes responsibility and discipline. It takes attention and keen observation. It takes time and practice – a lot of doing it wrong before you get it right. And it takes listening to your own intuition.

Notice how often I repeat 'it takes'. In the beginning, there's a lot of 'take' and very little 'give' on your baby's part.

Every baby is different, which is why I tell my mums that their first job is to understand the baby they have, not the one they dreamed about during the nine months of pregnancy.

Coming Home

Because I see myself as an advocate for the whole family, not just the new baby, part of my job is to help parents gain perspective. I tell mums and dads right from the start: this won't last for ever. You will calm down. You will become more confident. And at some point, believe it or not, your baby will sleep through the night. For now, though, you must lower your expectations. You'll have good days and not-so-good days; be prepared for both.

The more organised you are before you come home, the happier everyone will be afterwards.

Arriving home

I advise a slow re-entry. When you walk through the door, take a deep, centring breath. Keep it simple. Start the dialogue by giving your baby a tour of the house. That's right, a tour, as if you're the curator of a museum and she's a distinguished visitor. Walk around with her in your arms and show her where she's going to live. Talk to her. In a soft, gentle voice, explain each room: 'Here's the kitchen. It's where Dad and I cook. This is the bathroom, where we have showers.' And so on. You might feel silly. Many new parents are shy when they first start to have a dialogue with their baby. That's okay. Practise, and you'll be amazed at how easy it becomes. Remember to respect your baby. You need to treat your little darling like a human being, as someone who can understand and feel. Granted, she speaks a language you may not yet understand, but it's nevertheless important to call her by name and to make every interaction a dialogue, not a lecture.

When you rock your baby, sway backwards and forwards, not side to side or up and down. Before your baby was born, she sloshed around inside you front to back as you walked, so she's used to, and comforted by, that kind of movement.

Limit visitors. Convince all but a few very close relatives and friends to stay away for the first few days. If parents are in from out of town, the greatest favours they can do for you are cooking, cleaning, and running errands. Let them know, in a kind way, that you'll ask for their help with the baby if you need it, but that you'd like to use this time to get to know your little one on your own. While you're walking around, Dad or Grandma could perhaps make some camomile tea or another calming beverage.

Give your baby a sponge bath and a feed. Keep in mind that you're not the only one in shock. Your baby has had quite a journey himself. This is a perfect opportunity for you to pore over your miracle of nature. It may be the first time you see your baby naked. Get acquainted with his bits and pieces. Explore each tiny finger and toe. Keep talking to him. Bond with him. Nurse him or give him a bottle. Watch him as he gets sleepy. Start him off right, and allow him to fall asleep in his own cot or moses basket. Hospital nurseries are kept

Homecoming Checklist

• Put sheets on the cot, crib or moses basket.

• Set up the changing table. Have everything you need – wipes, nappies, cotton wool, etc – within easy reach.

• Have baby's first wardrobe ready. Take everything out of the packages, remove any tags, and wash in a mild detergent that has no bleach.

• Stock your fridge and freezer. A week or two before you're due, make a lasagne, a shepherd's pie, soups and other dishes that freeze well. Make sure you have all the staples on hand – milk, butter, eggs, cereal, pet food. You'll eat better and more cheaply, and will avoid frantic trips to the shops.

• Don't take too much to the hospital. Remember, you'll have several extra bags – and the baby – to bring home.

quite warm, almost womb-like, so make sure the temperature in the baby's new 'woom' is around 22°C (72°F).

Take small bites
You've got a lot on your plate; don't heap on any additional pressures. Give yourself a manageable number of daily goals and prioritise your

tasks by creating piles marked 'urgent', 'do later', and 'can wait till I feel better'. If you're calm and honest when you assess each chore, you'll be surprised at how much goes in that last pile.

It is also important during the early days to take naps during the day. When the baby sleeps, take advantage of it. Babies take a few days to recuperate from the shock of birth. It's not unusual for a one- or two-day-old newborn to sleep for six hours at a stretch, which gives you a little time to recuperate from your own trauma.

A word about pets
Animals can get jealous of new babies – after all, it's like bringing another child home. I advise parents never to leave a baby alone with any pet.

Dogs
You can't actually talk to your dog to prepare it, but you can bring home a blanket or nappy from the hospital to get it used to the baby's smell. When you come home from the hospital, get Rover to meet the new arrival outside the house, before you go in. Dogs are very territorial and likely not to welcome a stranger. It helps if they've become accustomed to the baby's scent.

Cats
It's an old wives' tale that cats like to lie on babies' faces, but cats are certainly attracted to that little lump of warmth. Keeping the cat out of the nursery is the best way to prevent it from jumping into the cot and curling up with your baby. Your baby's lungs are very tender. Cat hair and fine dog hair, such as that on a Jack Russell, can cause an allergic reaction, and even bring on asthma.

Getting to Know Your Baby

In my experience, I've found that infants generally fit into one of five broad temperamental types, which I call *Angel*, *Textbook*, *Touchy*, *Spirited* and *Grumpy*. I describe each below. To help you look at your baby, I've made up a 20-item multiple-choice test that applies to healthy babies from five days old to eight months. Bear in mind that during the first two weeks, there may be apparent changes in temperament that are actually quite temporary. For example, circumcision (often done on the eighth day) or any type of birth abnormality such as jaundice (which makes babies sleepy) may obscure a baby's true nature.

I suggest that both you and your partner answer the questions separately. If you're a single mum or dad, enlist the cooperation of your own parent, a sibling or other relative, a good friend, a childcare worker – in short, anyone who has spent time around your baby.

The know-your-baby quiz
For each of the following questions, pick the best answer – in other words, the statement that describes your child most of the time.

1. My baby
    A.   rarely cries
    B.   cries only when she's hungry, tired or over-stimulated
    C.   cries for no apparent reason
    D.   cries very loudly, and if I don't attend to it, she quickly gets into a rage cry
    E.   cries a lot of the time

2. When it's time for him to go to sleep, my baby
    A.   lies peacefully in his crib and drifts off to sleep
    B.   generally falls asleep easily within 20 minutes
    C.   fusses a bit and seems to be drifting off, but then keeps waking up
    D.   is very restless and often needs to be swaddled or held
    E.   cries a lot and seems to resent being put down

3. When she wakes up in the morning, my baby
    A.   rarely cries – she plays in her crib until I come in
    B.   coos and looks around
    C.   needs immediate attention or she starts crying
    D.   screams
    E.   whimpers

4. When I take my baby on any kind of outing, he
    A. is extremely portable
    B. is okay as long as where I take him isn't too busy or unfamiliar
    C. fusses a great deal
    D. is very demanding of my attention
    E. doesn't like to be handled a lot

5. When confronted by a friendly stranger cooing at her, my baby
    A. immediately smiles
    B. takes a moment and then usually smiles fairly quickly
    C. is likely to cry at first, unless the stranger can win her over
    D. gets very excited
    E. hardly ever smiles

6. When there's a loud noise, like a dog barking or a slamming door,
   my baby
    A. is never rattled
    B. notices it but isn't bothered
    C. flinches visibly and often starts to cry
    D. gets loud himself
    E. starts to cry

7. When I first gave my baby a bath, she
    A. took to the water like a duck
    B. was a little surprised at the sensation, but liked it almost
        immediately
    C. was very sensitive – she shook a little and seemed afraid
    D. was wild – flailing about and splashing
    E. hated it and cried

8. My baby's body language is typically
   A. relaxed and alert almost always
   B. relaxed most of the time
   C. tense and very reactive to external stimuli
   D. jerky – his arms and legs are often flailing all over the place
   E. rigid – arms and legs are often fairly stiff

9. When I change my baby's nappy, bathe her or dress her, she
   A. always takes it in her stride
   B. is okay if I do it slowly and let her know what I'm doing
   C. is often cranky, as if she can't stand being naked
   D. wriggles a lot and tries to pull everything off the changing table
   E. hates it – dressing is always a battle

10. If I suddenly bring my baby into bright light, like sunlight or fluorescent light, he
    A. takes it in his stride
    B. can sometimes act startled
    C. blinks excessively or tries to turn his head away from the light
    D. becomes over-stimulated
    E. acts annoyed

11a. *If you bottle-feed.* When I feed my baby, she
    A. always sucks properly, pays attention, and usually feeds within 20 minutes
    B. is a little erratic during growth spurts but generally a good feeder

    C. is very squirmy and takes a long time to finish the bottle
    D. grabs at the bottle aggressively and tends to over-eat
    E. is often cranky and feedings take a long time

11b. *If you breastfeed.* When I feed my baby, he
    A. latches on immediately – it was a snap right from day one
    B. took a day or two to latch on properly, but now we do fine
    C. always wants to suckle but goes on and off the breast, as if he's forgotten how to nurse
    D. eats well as long as I hold him the way he wants me to
    E. gets very annoyed and restless, as if I don't have enough milk for him

12. The comment that best describes the communication between my baby and me is
    A. she always lets me know exactly what she needs
    B. most of the time her cues are easy to read
    C. she confuses me; sometimes she even cries at me
    D. she asserts her likes and dislikes very clearly and often loudly
    E. she usually gets my attention with loud, angry crying

13. My baby
    A. can amuse herself for long periods by staring at anything, even the slats in the crib
    B. can play on her own for around 15 minutes
    C. finds it hard to be amused in unfamiliar surroundings
    D. needs a lot of stimulation to be amused
    E. is not easily amused by anything

14. My baby seems to
    A. feel utterly safe in her cot
    B. prefer her cot most of the time
    C. feel insecure in her cot
    D. act feisty, like her cot is a prison
    E. resent being put down into her cot

15. A comment that best describes my baby is that
    A. you hardly know there's a baby in the house – he's good as gold
    B. he's easy to handle, easy to predict
    C. he's a very delicate little thing
    D. I fear when he begins crawling, he's going to get into everything
    E. he's an 'old soul' – he acts like he's been here before

To score the self-test above, count how many times you've used A, B, C, D or E. Each letter denotes a corresponding type:

As = Angel baby
Bs = Textbook baby
Cs = Touchy baby
Ds = Spirited baby
Es = Grumpy baby

Zeroing in on your baby's type

When you tally up your letters, chances are that you'll have picked predominantly one or two. Perhaps she's a bit like this, a bit like that. Read all five descriptions. I've exemplified each profile with a baby I've met who fits it almost exactly.

The Angel baby

As you might expect, this is the kind of baby every first-time-pregnant woman imagines herself to have: as good as gold. She is mellow, eternally smiling and consistently undemanding. Her cues are easy to read. She's not bothered by new surroundings and is extremely portable – in fact, you can take her anywhere. She feeds, plays and sleeps easily, and usually doesn't cry when she wakes up.

The Textbook baby

This is our predictable baby, and, as such, he's fairly easy to handle. He does everything on cue, so there are few surprises. He reaches all the milestones right on schedule – sleeps through the night by three months, rolls over by five, sits up by six. He'll have growth spurts like clockwork – periods during which his appetite will suddenly increase because he's putting on extra body weight or making a developmental leap. It's not hard to get him to sleep, either.

The Touchy baby

For an ultra-sensitive baby the world is an endless array of sensory challenges. He flinches at the sound of a motorcycle revving outside his window, the TV blaring, a dog barking in the house next door. He blinks or turns his head away from bright light. He sometimes cries for no apparent reason, even at his mother. He also nurses erratically, sometimes acting as though he's forgotten how. At naptime and at night, he often has difficulty falling asleep. Touchy babies easily get off schedule, because their systems are so fragile. When you have a Touchy baby, the quicker you learn his cues and his cries, the simpler life is. These babies love structure and predictability.

The Spirited baby

This is a baby who seems to emerge from the womb knowing what she likes and doesn't like, and won't hesitate to let you know it. Babies like this are very vocal and even seem aggressive at times. She often screams for Mum or Dad when she gets up in the morning. Indeed, she babbles a lot and loudly. Her body language tends to be a bit jerky. She often needs swaddling to get to sleep, because her flailing arms and legs keep her up and over-stimulated. If she starts crying and the cycle is not interrupted, it's like a point of no return, and her crying leads to more crying until she's reached a fever pitch of rage.

The Grumpy baby

I have a theory that babies like this have been here before – they're old souls, as we call them – and they're not all that happy to be back. I may be wrong, of course, but whatever the reason, I assure you this type of baby is downright mardy, as we say in Yorkshire. He's mad at the world and lets you know it. He whimpers every morning, doesn't smile much during the day, and fusses his way to sleep every night. His mum has a lot of trouble keeping baby-sitters, because they tend to take this little guy's bad humour personally. He hates baths at first, and every time someone tries to change or dress him, he's fidgety and irritable. To calm a Grumpy baby, it usually takes a patient mum or dad, because these babies get very angry and their cries are particularly loud and long. The 'sh... sh... sh...' has to be louder than the cry.

Love at First Sight?

Eyes meet across the room and you're instantly in love – or at least that's how it happens in Hollywood. But it's not like this for many real couples. It's the same way with mothers and their babies. Some mums are instantly in love, but for many it takes a while. You're exhausted, shocked and frightened, and, perhaps most difficult of all, you want it to be perfect. It rarely is. So don't get down on yourself. Loving your baby takes time. Just as it happens with adults, true love comes as you get to know the person.

Mums, it helps to talk to anyone who can remind you that the ups and downs are normal – good friends who've been through it, sisters, and your own mother if you have a good relationship with her.

Fantasy Versus Reality

There are two critical aspects of baby whispering: respect and common sense. Just as you can't apply blanket prescriptions to all people, the same is true with babies.

Forget about wishful thinking. You must deal with the reality of who your child is – and know what's best for your child. And I promise that if you watch and listen carefully, your baby will tell you precisely what he needs and how to help him through difficult situations. Ultimately, that kind of empathy and understanding will make your child's life a bit easier, because you'll help him build on his strengths and compensate for his weaknesses.

And no matter what kind of baby you have, all infants do better when life is calm and predictable. To get started straight away with a routine that will help your whole family thrive, see Chapter 4, 'The E.A.S.Y. Routine'.

CHAPTER TWO
The Baby Essentials

The following essentials may seem fairly obvious, but, like everything with babies, sometimes it's the little things that make all the difference.

Changing Nappies

Most babies cry on the changing table because they don't know what's happening to them and/or they don't like it – not one bit.

- When I change a baby's nappy, I try to maintain a steady dialogue. I bend down, putting my face around 30–35cm (12–14in) from hers – straight on, never at an angle, because babies see better that way – and I talk her through the process.

- It may take you a few weeks to get the hang of it, but you should strive for a five-minute nappy change. The key is to have everything ready – tops of the cream and wipes open, nappy unfolded and ready to slip under baby's bottom, your wastebasket open and ready for the dirty nappy.

- For the first three or four weeks, invest in some inexpensive nightgowns that tie or snap down the front and are open at the bottom, providing easy access for changing nappies. In the beginning, you're bound to have a few leaky nappies every now and then. Having a pile of extra nighties on hand saves time and worry.

- When you first lay baby down for a nappy change, slip a clean nappy under his bottom. Open the soiled nappy but don't remove it until you've cleaned the genital and anal areas. When you're finished, remove the old nappy and the new one will be right where you need it.

- When all the tricks of the trade fail to calm a baby, try changing him in your lap – many babies prefer it, and it saves you the trouble of standing over a changing table.

Dressing

To avoid a struggle I urge parents to buy simple clothes. Buy tops with snaps up the front, one-piece outfits with snaps down the body or with Velcro closures on the shoulder. Always go for ease and convenience rather than style. I would definitely suggest not buying shirts or tops that have to go over a baby's head.

However, if you've already bought shirts or tops for your baby that go over her head, here's the best way to avoid a battle:

- Lie her down on her back.
- Scrunch the material up and stretch the neck wide. Go from under your baby's chin, quickly over her face, and to the back of her head.
- Push your own fingers through the armholes first and then grab hold of your baby's hand. Pull it through the armhole, like you're threading a needle.

Washing

After a hard day eating, sleeping and playing, your baby deserves a little rest and relaxation in the form of a massage, bath or sponge-wash.

Your baby's first bath will come at around 14 days, time enough for the umbilical cord to fall off. Before that, you will sponge-wash your baby. Remember, take care to see the experience from your baby's perspective. It should be a fun, interactive time, lasting 15 to 20 minutes depending on your patience and your baby's tolerance, and try always to take the gentlest route.

Sponging suggestions

- Have everything you need – washcloths, warm water, cotton wool balls, ointment and towel – close by and ready to use.
- Keep baby warmly wrapped. Going from head to toe, wash one part of her body at a time; pat dry and move on.
- Use a small washcloth to clean the groin area; always wipe away from the genitals towards the anus.
- To clean the eyes, use a cotton wool ball, one ball per eye, sweeping outwards from the corner closest to the nose.
- To clean the cord stump, use a cotton swab dipped in surgical spirit. Go right to the base. Babies sometimes cry, although it doesn't hurt; it just feels cold.
- If your baby boy has been circumcised, keep the incision moist and protected against urine by covering it with a Vaseline-smeared piece of gauze or cotton. Don't put any water on your baby's penis until it has healed.

Bathing

The ideal time is before bed, because it's the best way to wind down. It's also one of the most special parent–child experiences, often Dad's favourite chore.

As with sponge baths, make sure you have everything to hand before you begin, so that there's a minimum of fumbling when you take your slippery baby out of the water.

Bath essentials

- flat-bottomed plastic bath (I like to prop it on a bath stand rather than the floor, because that's easier on one's back, and because the stands usually have drawers and a shelf to keep everything within easy reach)
- jug of warm, clean water
- liquid baby wash
- two washcloths
- hooded or over-sized towel
- clothes and fresh nappy ready on the changing table

My ten-step guide to bathing

Please do remember that you have to maintain a dialogue with your baby throughout. Keep talking. Listen and watch for his response, and continue to tell him what you're doing.

1. *Set the mood.* Make sure the room is warm, around 22–4°C (72–5°F). Put on music – any kind of gentle pop music (it's to help you relax as well).
2. *Fill the bath two-thirds full.* Put a capful of baby wash directly into the water. The temperature should be around 38°C (100°F), slightly warmer than body temperature. Test the water on the inside of your wrist, never your hand; the water should feel warm, not hot, because baby's skin is more sensitive than yours.
3. *Pick up your baby.* Place the palm of your right hand on your baby's chest, and scissor your fingers so that three fingers go under his left armpit and your thumb and index finger rest on his chest. (Reverse that if you're a lefty.) Slide your left hand behind his neck and

shoulders and gently bend his body forward, transferring the weight of his body on to your right hand. Now place your left hand under his bum and lift. With him slumped over your right hand, he's now in a sitting position, bent forward slightly and perched on your left hand. Never lower a baby into the bath on his back. It's disorienting to an infant, like going backwards off a diving board.

4. *Put him in the bath.* Slowly lower him into the bath in that sitting position, his feet first and then his bum. Then transfer your left hand to the back of his head and neck to support him. Very slowly ease him back into the water. Now your right hand is free. Use it to put a wet washcloth on his chest to keep him warm.

5. *Don't use soap directly on baby's skin.* Remember that you've put some baby wash in the water. With your fingers, wipe his neck and groin area. Lift his legs a bit so you can get to his bottom. Then take a little jug and pour the water over his body to rinse the soapy water off. He hasn't been playing in the sandbox, so he's not really dirty. His bath at this point is more for establishing a routine than for cleanliness.

6. *Use a washcloth around his head to wash his hair.* Very often babies haven't got much hair. Even if they do, they don't need a shampoo and set. Take the open washcloth and wipe it around his scalp. Pour fresh water to rinse, taking care not to get water in his eyes.

7. *Don't get water in his ears.* Make sure the hand that's supporting his back doesn't dip too low in the water.

8. *Get ready to end the bath.* With your free hand, grab the hooded towel (or an oversized towel without a hood). Put the hood (or the corner of the oversized towel) between your teeth and tuck the ends under your armpits.

9. *Take the baby out.* Carefully shift your baby into the sitting position you used at the beginning of the bath. Most of his weight should be on your right hand, which, with fingers scissored, is supporting his chest. Lift him up, his back towards you, and place his head in the centre of your chest a little under where the hood, or the corner of the big towel, is. Wrap the ends of the towel around his body and flop the hood or towel corner over his head.

10. *Take him to the changing table to get dressed.* Do it exactly the same way for the first three months. There's security in repetition. In time, depending on your baby's nature, instead of getting him into his babygro or nightie straight away, you can add a massage to this time of relaxation.

> Never leave a baby unattended in a bathtub. If by chance you've forgotten the baby wash, just rinse him or her with clear water this time, and remember to have everything ready for the next bath.

If your baby cries at bath time and you've taken care to follow the steps, which will make the experience safe, slow and enjoyable, it's probably a matter of your baby's sensitivities and temperament rather than anything you've done. If he seems chronically distressed at bath time, it's best to wait a few days and then try again. If he is still upset, which may be the case if you have a Touchy baby, you may have to continue to sponge-bathe for the first month or two – and there's nothing wrong with that. You've got to read your baby. If he's telling you, 'I don't like what you're doing – I can't tolerate it,' you must wait.

Massage

Controlled stimulation can speed the development of the brain and nervous system, improve circulation, tone muscles, and reduce stress and irritability. Massage has emerged as a wonderful way to support infant health and growth. It teaches babies to appreciate the power of touch. Babies who've been massaged seem to feel more comfortable with their own bodies as they grow into toddlerhood.

Three months old is an optimal time to begin giving your baby massages. Start slowly and pick a time when you're not rushed or preoccupied, so that you're 100 per cent involved in the experience. You can't speed through the process or do it half-heartedly. And don't expect your baby to lie there for 15 minutes the first time you try it. Rather, start with a three-minute rub and build up to progressively longer sessions. I love to combine massage with the evening bath, because it's so relaxing for both the adult and the baby. But whenever you have time is the right time. Please do also take into consideration that some infants take to massage better than others.

Massage essentials

You can use either the floor or a changing table; choose a position that's comfortable for you, too. You'll also need:

- a pillow
- a waterproof pad
- two fluffy bath towels
- baby oil, vegetable oil or specially formulated baby massage oil (never use a scented aromatherapy oil, which is too strong for baby's skin and too pungent for his sense of smell)

Ten steps to a more relaxed baby

Make sure you have everything that you need to hand (see above, 'Massage essentials'). Remember to go slowly, to tell your baby before you touch her what you're going to do, and to explain each step along the way. If at any time your infant seems uncomfortable (you don't have to wait for a cry; her squirming will tell you), that's the time to stop the massage. Don't expect your baby to lie there for a full-body massage the first time you try this. You'll have to build tolerance a few minutes at a time. Start with a few movements, lasting only two or three minutes. Over several weeks, or longer, work up to 15 or 20 minutes.

1. *Make sure the environment is conducive.* The room should be warm, around 24°C (75°F), with no draughts. Put on soft music. Your 'massage table' will consist of a waterproof pad placed on top of a pillow; over that, lay a fluffy bath towel.

2. *Prepare for the experience.* Ask yourself, 'Can I really be in the here and now with my baby, or is there another better time for me to do this?' If you're certain that you can give fully of yourself, wash your hands and take a few deep, centring breaths to relax. Then prepare your baby. Lay her down. Talk to her. Explain, 'We're going to give your little body a massage.' As you're explaining what you're about to do, put a small amount of oil (a teaspoon or two) into your hands and briskly rub your palms together to warm the oil.

3. *Ask permission to begin.* You will begin at your baby's feet and work your way up to his head. Before you even touch your baby, though, explain, 'I'm going to pick up your little foot now. I'm just going to stroke the bottom of it.'

4. *Legs and feet first*. On her feet, use a thumb-over-thumb movement – one thumb rubs the foot upward, taking turns with the other thumb, which moves in the same direction. Gently stroke the sole of her foot, heel towards toe. Press in all over the bottom of the foot. Squeeze each toe delicately. You can say the nursery rhyme 'This little piggy...' while you're doing each toe. Massage over the top of the foot towards the ankle. Make small circles around the ankle. As you go up the leg, gently do the 'rope twist'. First, wrap your hands loosely around your baby's legs. As you move your top hand towards the left, move your bottom hand towards the right, in effect gently 'twisting' his skin and muscles and thereby increasing the circulation in his legs. Do this all the way up each leg. Then slip your hands under your baby's bottom and massage both buttocks, stroking the legs down to the feet.

5. *Stomach next*. Put your hands on the baby's tummy and make gentle sweeping motions outwards. Using both thumbs, gently massage from the belly button towards the outside. 'Walk' your fingers from the stomach to the chest.

6. *Chest*. Say 'I love you' and make a 'sun-and-moon' motion by using both of your index fingers to trace a circle – the 'sun' – that starts at the top of your baby's chest and ends around his belly button. Now take your right hand and go back up, tracing a 'moon' (a backward C) up to the top of his chest; then do the same with your left hand (a forward C). Repeat this a few times. Then do a heart-shape movement – with all your fingers on the chest, at the centre of his breastbone, gently trace a heart, ending at his belly button.

7. *Arms and hands*. Massage under the arm. Do the rope-twist movement, then do open-hand massage on both arms. Roll each

finger and repeat the 'This little piggy' rhyme, this time with the fingers. On the top of the hand, make small circles around the wrist.

8. *Face.* Take care to be extra gentle around the face. Massage the forehead and eyebrows, and use your thumbs around the eye area. Go down the bridge of your baby's nose, back and forth across the cheek, from her ears towards her upper and lower lips and back. Make small circles around the jaw and behind her ears. Rub her earlobes and under her chin. Now gently turn her over.

9. *Head and back.* Make circles on the back of your baby's head and shoulders. Using a back-and-forth motion, stroke him up and down. Make small circles along the back muscles, which are parallel to the spinal column. Allow your hands to travel the full length of his body, from the top of his back all the way down to his bottom and then to his ankles.

10. *End the massage.* 'We're all done now, darling. Don't you feel good?' If you follow the above steps every time, your baby will look forward to the experience.

Throughout the massage, remember to respect your baby's sensitivities. Never continue with a massage if she cries; let a few weeks go by and try again, this time for an even shorter period. I can only assure you that if you can get your baby used to the joy of touch, she will not only benefit in the long run, it will also be easier for her to get to sleep.

CHAPTER THREE
Understanding Your Baby

When parents ask me to help figure out why their baby is fussing or crying, I know they are anxious and want me to do something immediately. Much to their surprise, however, I say, 'Stop. Let's try to figure out what he's saying to us!'

- I first hang back a bit in order to watch the little one's movements – the flailing arms and legs, the little tongue curling and darting in and out of his tiny mouth, the back arching. Each gesture means something.
- I pay close attention to the kind of cries and sounds he's making. Pitch, intensity and frequency are all parts of baby language.
- I also absorb the surroundings. I imagine what it's like to be that baby. Besides paying attention to his overall appearance, his sounds and gestures, I look around the room, feel the temperature, and listen to the noises of the household.
- I observe how his mum and dad look – nervous, tired or angry – and I listen to what they're saying. I might ask a few questions as well, such as: 'When did you last feed him?'

S.L.O.W.

Whenever your baby fusses or cries, try this simple strategy, which takes only a few seconds:

- *Stop.* Remember that crying is your baby's language.
- *Listen.* What does this particular cry mean?
- *Observe.* What is your baby doing? What else is going on?
- *What's Up?* Based on what you hear and see, evaluate and respond.

Why stop?

When your baby cries, your natural inclination may be to rescue. You may believe that your infant is in distress; worse, you may think that crying is bad. The S in S.L.O.W. reminds you to curb those feelings and, instead, hold back for a moment. Let me explain.

Your baby must be allowed to develop his or her 'voice'

By rushing in, a parent unwittingly trains her infant not to have a voice. When parents don't stop really to listen and learn how to distinguish different cries, those cries, which numerous studies have proven are differentiated at birth, in time actually become indistinguishable. In other words, when a baby is not responded to at all, or if every cry is 'answered' with food, baby learns that it doesn't matter how she cries – it always results in the same outcome. Eventually, she gives up and all her cries will sound the same.

You need to foster your baby's self-soothing skills

Among other purposes, crying is a way of blocking out external stimulation, which is why babies cry when they're over-tired. Now, I'm not advocating that we let infants cry themselves to sleep – far from it. I think that's both unresponsive and cruel. But we can use their 'tired' cries as cues; we can darken their rooms, shield them from light and sound. Moreover, sometimes an infant will cry for a few seconds – I call it the 'phantom baby' cry – and then put himself back to sleep. He has essentially soothed himself. If we rush in, then he quickly loses that ability.

You must learn your baby's language
S.L.O.W. is a tool that helps you get to know your baby and understand what she needs. By holding back, waiting to distinguish the cry and the body language that goes with it, you can meet your baby's requirements more appropriately than you would if you just shoved a breast in her mouth or kept rocking her without really understanding her need. I must once again stress, though, that stopping for a few seconds to go through this mental evaluation process does not mean letting your baby cry it out. You're just taking a moment to learn her language.

Listening
It will take a little practice to distinguish your baby's different types of cries, but remember that the L in S.L.O.W. – listening – involves also paying attention to the broader picture to find clues of meaning. Here are some tips that will help you listen more intently:

Consider the time of day
At what point in the day did your baby start to fuss or cry? Had she just eaten? Had she been up playing? Sleeping? Might her nappy be wet or dirty? Might she be over-stimulated? In your mind, play back what happened earlier or even yesterday. Did your baby do something new, like roll over for the first time or start to crawl?

Consider the context
What else had been happening in the household? Had the dog been barking? Had anyone been using the vacuum cleaner or any other loud appliances? Was there a great deal of noise outside? Babies are very sensitive to odours. Also consider the temperature in the room.

Consider yourself

Babies absorb an adult's emotions, particularly their mum's. If you're feeling more anxious or tired or angry than usual, this could affect your baby. Or perhaps you had an upsetting phone call or were yelling at someone. If you then nursed your baby, he most assuredly would feel the difference in your demeanour.

Crying danger signals

Crying is normal and healthy. But you should call your doctor if:

- a typically content baby cries for two hours or more
- excessive crying is accompanied by
    fever
    vomiting
    diarrhoea
    convulsions
    limpness
    pale or blue skin
    unusual bruising or rash
- your child never cries, or if his cry is extremely weak
  and sounds more like that of a kitten than a baby

Why it's sometimes hard to listen

There are a number of reasons why parents sometimes find it hard to listen to a crying baby and to be objective about what they hear. Perhaps one or more of the following rings true for you. If so, at first you might have trouble with the L in S.L.O.W. Take heart: being aware is often all it takes to change your perspective.

1. *You have someone else's voice in your head.* It may be your parents or your friends, or a particular baby-care expert whom you saw or heard in the media. Become aware of the 'shoulds' you harbour and know that you don't have to obey them. They might be right for someone else's baby, someone else's family, but not for you. The true joy of parenting comes when we are empowered and can follow our own inner voice of guidance. Keep your eyes open, become informed; consider all options, all styles of parenting. Then make decisions about what's right for you and your family.

2. *You attribute adult emotions and intentions to your crying baby.* It is important to remember that they're not crying to manipulate others. They don't want to get back at you or purposely ruin your day or evening. They're just babies – and they're pretty simple at that. Crying is their way of telling you, 'I need to go to sleep,' or 'I'm hungry,' or 'I've had enough,' or 'I'm a little chilly.' If you find yourself projecting adult emotions or intentions on to your baby, think of your little one as you would a barking puppy or a mewing kitten. You wouldn't assume that either of them was suffering, would you? You'd just think they were 'talking' to you. Do the same with your baby.

3. *You project your own motives or problems on to your baby.* Personal hang-ups can weaken one's powers of observation. The remedy is to know your own Achilles' heel and, through this awareness, stop yourself from imagining your worst nightmare whenever your child cries.

4. *You have a low level of tolerance for the sound of crying.* Remember, whenever a baby cries, to most people it feels twice as long. If you are particularly sensitive to noise, you might need to work on

> Always take a moment to ask yourself, 'Am I really tuning in to what my baby needs, or am I reacting to my own emotions?'

acceptance. Tell yourself: this is my life right now. I have a baby, and babies cry. It won't last for ever. The faster you learn his language, the less he'll cry, but he will still cry. In the meantime, don't put a negative spin on it. Also, get yourself a pair of earplugs or use your iPod; neither will prevent you from hearing your baby, but they will mute the sound a bit. As a friend observed, 'I'd much rather listen to Mozart than to the sound of crying.'

5. *You're embarrassed by your baby's crying.* This all-too-common feeling, I must say, seems to afflict women more than men. The following also bears repeating, so I'm directing my publisher to print it in bold letters for all mums to see (make signs like this and hang them all over the house, in your car and office, and slip one into your handbag, too): **A CRYING BABY DOES NOT EQUAL A BAD PARENT**.

   Also remember that you and your child are two separate people – don't take his or her crying personally. It has nothing to do with you.

6. *You had a difficult delivery.* I've observed this lingering sadness and regret in some mothers. Instead of focusing on the new baby, they get stuck feeling sorry for themselves, because reality didn't live up to their expectations. They tend to replay the delivery in their mind. They feel guilty, especially if the baby had a problem – and they feel helpless. But because they're not aware of what's really going on in their psyches, they can't get past it. If more than two months has passed since your delivery and you find yourself going over the event repeatedly in your mind, or telling the story to

anyone who's willing to listen, try to think or talk about it in a new way. Instead of focusing on the 'poor baby', admit your own disappointment.

Sharpening your powers of observation: a head-to-toe guide

Along with the sound of a baby's crying come gestures, facial expressions and body postures. 'Reading' your baby involves almost all your sensory organs – your ears, eyes, fingers, nose – as well as your mind, which helps you put it all together. In order to help parents with the O in S.L.O.W., which enables them to interpret their baby's body language, I've taken a mental inventory of the many babies I've known and cared for. Aside from what their cries sound like, I asked myself what they looked like when they were hungry, tired, distressed, hot, cold or wet. I imagined my tiny wards on videotape with the sound off, which forced me to zoom in on what their faces and bodies looked like.

Below is a head-to-toe view of what I saw in my imaginary video. Note that this body language is 'spoken' by infants until they're five or six months old, at which point they begin to have more control over their bodies – for example, they may suck a finger to self-soothe.

> When out of the house, it's a good idea to take a pushchair or moses basket with you so that you have a handy and safe place for a tired baby to sleep.

Body Language	Translation
Head	
⇨ moves from side to side	⇨ tired
⇨ turns away from object	⇨ needs a change of scenery
⇨ turns to side and cranes neck back (mouth agape)	⇨ hungry
⇨ if in an upright position, nods, like a person falling asleep on a subway	⇨ tired
Eyes	
⇨ red, bloodshot	⇨ tired
⇨ slowly close and spring open; slowly close again and spring open again – and again	⇨ tired
⇨ 'seven-mile stare' – eyes wide, and unblinking, as if they're propped open with toothpicks	⇨ over-tired; over-stimulated
Mouth/lips/tongue	
⇨ yawn	⇨ tired
⇨ lips pursed	⇨ hungry
⇨ the appearance of a scream but no sound comes out; finally, a gasp precedes an audible wail	⇨ has wind or other pain
⇨ bottom lip quivers	⇨ cold
⇨ sucks tongue	⇨ self-soothing, sometimes mistaken for hunger

Body Language	Translation
⇨ curls tongue at the sides	⇨ hungry – the classic 'rooting' gesture
⇨ curls tongue upward, like a little lizard; not accompanied by sucking	⇨ has wind or other pain

Face

⇨ grimacing, often scrunched up, like chewed toffee; if lying down, may also start to pant, roll her eyes, and make an expression that resembles a smile	⇨ has wind or other pain; or is having a bowel movement
⇨ red; veins at temples may stand out	⇨ left to cry too long; caused by holding breath; blood vessels expand

Hands/arms

⇨ hands brought up to mouth, trying to suck them	⇨ hungry, if baby hasn't eaten in 2½ to 3 hours; otherwise, needs to suckle
⇨ playing with fingers	⇨ needs a change of scenery
⇨ flailing and very uncoordinated, may claw at skin	⇨ over-tired; or has wind
⇨ arms shaking, slight tremor	⇨ has wind or other pain

Torso

⇨ arches back, looking for breast or bottle	⇨ hunger
⇨ squirms, moving bottom from side to side	⇨ wet nappy or cold; could also be wind

Body Language	Translation
⇨ goes rigid	⇨ has wind or other pain
⇨ shivers	⇨ cold
Skin	
⇨ clammy, sweaty	⇨ over-heated; or has been left to cry too long, which also causes body to expel heat and energy
⇨ bluish extremities	⇨ cold, or has wind or other pain and has been left to cry too long; as body expels heat and energy, blood is drained from extremities
⇨ tiny goose pimples	⇨ cold
Legs	
⇨ strong, uncoordinated kicking	⇨ tired
⇨ pulled up to chest	⇨ has wind or other abdominal pain

What's up?

In order for you to proceed to the W in S.L.O.W., which directs you to put it all together and figure out what's up, you can refer to the chart below which will help you evaluate the sounds and movements your baby makes. Every infant is unique, of course, but there are a number of universal signs that usually tell us what a baby needs. If you pay attention, you'll begin to comprehend your baby's language. Most parents I've worked with learn to decode 'baby talk' within two weeks, although some take up to a month.

Cause	Listen	Observe	Other Ways to Evaluate / Comments
Tired or over-tired	Starts as cranky, irregular-frequency fussing, but if not stopped quickly, it escalates to an over-tired cry: first, three short wails followed by a hard cry, then two short breaths and a longer, even louder cry. Usually they cry and cry – and if left alone, will eventually fall asleep.	Blinks, yawns. If not put to bed, physical signs can include back arching, legs kicking, and arms flailing; may grab own ears or cheeks and scratch face (a reflex); if you're holding him, squirms and tries to turn into your body. If he continues to cry, his face will become bright red.	Of all cries, the most often misinterpreted for hunger. Therefore, pay close attention to when it occurs. It may come after playtime, or after someone has been cooing at baby. Squirming is often mistaken for colic.

Cause	Listen	Observe	Other Ways to Evaluate / Comments
Over-stimulated	Long, hard cry, similar to over-tired.	Arms and legs flail; turns head away from light; will turn away from anyone trying to play with him.	Usually comes when baby has had enough playing and adult keeps trying to amuse him.
Needs a change of scenery	Cranky fussing that starts with noises of annoyance rather than outright cries.	Turns away from object placed before her; plays with fingers.	If it gets worse when you change baby's position, then she might be tired and needs a nap.
Pain/wind	Unmistakable shrill, high-pitched scream that comes without warning; may hold breath between wails and then start again.	Whole body tenses and becomes rigid, which perpetuates cycle, because then air can't pass; pulls knees upward to chest, face is scrunched in an expression of pain, tongue wiggles upwards, like a little lizard.	All newborns swallow air, which can cause wind. Throughout the day you'll hear a tiny squeaky, wincing sound in the back of the throat – that's air swallowing. Wind also can be caused by irregular feeding patterns.

Cause	Listen	Observe	Other Ways to Evaluate / Comments

Anger – see 'Over-stimulated' and 'Tired'. Babies aren't really 'angry' – that's adult projection. They're just not being read correctly.

Cause	Listen	Observe	Other Ways to Evaluate / Comments
Hunger	Slight cough-like sound in the back of the throat; then out comes the first cry. It's short to begin with then more steady: *waa, waa, waa* rhythm.	Baby starts to subtly lick her lips and then 'root' – tongue starts coming out and turns head to side; pulls fist towards mouth.	The best way to discern hunger is to look at when baby last ate. If she's on E.A.S.Y., it removes some of the guesswork.
Too cold	Full-out crying with bottom lip quivering.	Tiny goosebumps on skin; may shiver; cold extremities (hands, feet and nose); skin can sometimes have bluish tinge.	Can happen with a newborn after a bath or when you're changing or dressing her.

Cause	Listen	Observe	Other Ways to Evaluate / Comments
Too hot	Fussy whine that sounds more like panting, low at first, about five minutes; if left alone, will eventually launch into a cry.	Feels hot and sweaty; flushed; pants instead of breathing regularly; may see red blotchiness on baby's face and upper torso.	Different from fever in that cry is similar to a pain cry; skin is dry, not clammy. (Take your baby's temperature to be sure.)
'Where did you go? I need a cuddle.'	Cooing sounds suddenly turn into little short *waas* that sound like a kitten; crying disappears the minute baby is picked up.	Looks around, trying to find you.	If you catch this straight away, you may not need to pick baby up. A pat on the back and soft words of reassurance work better because they foster independence.

Cause	Listen	Observe	Other Ways to Evaluate / Comments
Over-feeding	Fussing, even crying, after meal.	Spits up frequently.	This often occurs when sleepiness and over-stimulation are mistaken for hunger.
Bowel movement	Grunts or cries while feeding.	Squirms and bears down; stops nursing; has bowel movement.	May be mistaken for hunger; Mum often thinks she's 'doing something wrong'.

CHAPTER FOUR
The E.A.S.Y. Routine

E.A.S.Y. is an acronym for the structured routine that I establish with all my babies, ideally from day one. Think of it as a recurring period, more or less three hours long, in which each of the following segments occurs in this order:

E – Eating. Whether your baby is fed by the breast, the bottle, or both, nutrition is his primary need. Babies are little eating machines. Relative to their body weight, they eat two to three times the calories an obese person does!

A – Activity. Before the age of three months, your baby will probably be eating and sleeping 70 per cent of the time. When she's not, she'll be on the changing table, in the tub, cooing in her crib or on a blanket, in her carriage for a stroll, or looking out the window from her infant seat. Doesn't sound like much activity from our perspective, but it's what babies do.

S – Sleeping. Whether they sleep like a dream or in fits and starts, all babies need to learn how to get themselves to sleep in their own beds (to promote their independence).

Y – You. After all is said and done – that is, when baby is sleeping – it's your turn. Sound impossible or unreasonable? It's not. If you follow my E.A.S.Y. programme, every few hours there will be 'you' time to rest, rejuvenate and, once you've started to heal, to get things done. Remember that in the first six weeks – the postpartum period – you will need to recover physically and emotionally from the trauma of childbirth.

A Bird's-eye View of the E.A.S.Y. Method

On Demand	E.A.S.Y.	Schedule
Following whatever baby demands and feeding 10–12 times a day as baby cries.	Flexible but structured routine that spans a 2½–3-hour period of eating, activity, sleep and 'you' time.	Clock-watching to conform to a predetermined timetable of regular feedings, usually 3–4 hours apart.
Unpredictable – baby takes the lead.	Predictable – parents set a pace that baby can follow, and baby knows what to expect.	Predictable but anxiety-provoking – parents set a schedule, which baby may not follow.
Parents don't learn to interpret baby's signals; many cries misinterpreted as hunger.	Because it's logical, parents can anticipate baby's need and therefore are more likely to understand the different cries.	Cries may be ignored if they don't match schedule; parents don't learn to interpret baby's signals.
Parents have no life – baby sets the schedule.	Parents can plan their lives.	Parents are ruled by the clock.
Parents feel confused; there is often chaos in the house.	Parents feel more confident about their own parenting because they understand their child's cues and cries.	Parents often feel guilty, anxious, even angry if baby doesn't conform to the schedule.

Why E.A.S.Y. Works

Humans, at any age, are habitual creatures – they function better within a regular pattern of events. Structure and routine are normal to everyday life. Everything has a logical order. Babies need routines as much as we do, which is why E.A.S.Y. works.

- *Babies don't like surprises*. Their delicate systems do best when they eat, sleep and play pretty much at the same time every day, and in the same order. It may vary slightly, but not by much. Children, especially infants and babies, also like to know what's coming up next. They tend not to be good about hidden surprises.

- *E.A.S.Y. gets your baby used to the natural order of things – food, activity and rest*. I've seen parents put their infants to bed right after eating, often because the baby falls asleep on the breast or bottle. I don't advise this for two reasons: one, the baby becomes dependent on the bottle or breast, and soon needs it to fall asleep; two, do you want to sleep after every meal?

- *Structure and organisation give everyone in the family a sense of security*. A structured routine helps parents set a pace that their baby can follow and create an environment that helps him know what's coming. With E.A.S.Y., there is no rigidity – we listen to baby and respond to his specific needs – but we keep his day in logical order. We, not baby, set the stage.

- *E.A.S.Y. helps parents interpret their baby*. Because I've handled so many babies, I know their language. When a baby cries, 'I'm hungry – feed me,' it sounds different to my ear than 'My nappy's dirty – change me' or 'I'm tired – help me calm down and get to sleep.' My goal is to help parents learn how to listen and observe so that they, too, can understand the language of infancy. But this takes time, practice and a bit of trial and error. In the meantime, with E.A.S.Y., you can make intelligent guesses about what your baby wants even before you become fluent in baby language.

- *E.A.S.Y. establishes a solid but flexible foundation for your baby.* E.A.S.Y. sets up certain guidelines and routines that parents can adapt according to their baby's temperament and, just as important, their own needs. Although the same order – eat, activity and sleep – is always maintained, changes also occur as a baby gets older.
- *E.A.S.Y. facilitates cooperative parenting – with or without a partner.* When the primary caretaker of a newborn – usually Mum – doesn't have time for herself, she's likely to moan about it or resent her partner for not sharing the burden. I see these difficulties crop up in so many of the households I visit.

An E.A.S.Y. Timetable

All babies are different, but from birth to three months, the following routine is fairly typical. As your baby becomes a more efficient feeder and is content to play independently for longer periods, don't be afraid to adjust it.

- *Eating*: 25–40 minutes on breast or bottle; a normal baby, weighing 2.75kg (6lb) or more, can go 2½–3 hours to the next feed.
- *Activity*: 45 minutes (includes nappy-changing, dressing and, once a day, a nice bath).
- *Sleep*: 15 minutes to fall asleep; naps of half an hour to an hour; will go for progressively longer periods through the night after the first two or three weeks.
- *You*: an hour or more for you when the baby is asleep; this time is extended as baby gets older, takes less time to eat, plays independently, and takes longer naps.

> If you're a single parent, friends are a lifeline. For those who can't or don't want to help with childcare, enlist their support to help with the housework or grocery shopping and other errands. Remember that you have to ask. Don't expect others to read your mind and then become resentful when they don't.

Wingers and Planners

Some of us are planners by nature, others like to live on the edge and wing it, and most are somewhere in the middle. What about you? To find out, I've devised a brief questionnaire that can help you figure out where you fall on the Wing It / Plan It continuum. Each item is based on what I've seen in the homes of the many different families I've met in over 20 years of baby whispering. By observing how parents keep house and conduct their daily lives, I can pretty much tell how well they'll adapt to a structured routine once the baby arrives.

What's your WPQ (Wing It / Plan It Quotient)?

For each question, circle the number that best describes you. Use the following key:

5 = always
4 = usually yes
3 = sometimes
2 = usually no
1 = never

I live by a schedule.	5 4 3 2 1
I prefer people to call before they drop in.	5 4 3 2 1
After shopping or laundry, I immediately put everything away.	5 4 3 2 1
I prioritise my daily and weekly tasks.	5 4 3 2 1
My desk is very organised.	5 4 3 2 1
I shop weekly for the food and other supplies I know I'll need.	5 4 3 2 1

I hate it when people are late.	5	4	3	2	1
I am careful not to overbook myself.	5	4	3	2	1
Before starting a project, I lay out whatever I'm going to use.	5	4	3	2	1
I clean out and organise my wardrobe at regular intervals.	5	4	3	2	1
When I finish a chore, I put away whatever I was using.	5	4	3	2	1
I plan ahead.	5	4	3	2	1

To find out your WPQ, add up your scores and divide by 12. Your total score will range somewhere between 1 and 5, which indicates where you fall on the continuum.

Why is this important? If you're too much at either extreme, you might be one of those parents who initially has trouble with my E.A.S.Y. method, either because you're a bit on the rigid side or too laissez-faire. That doesn't mean you can't implement a structured routine, only that you might have to give a little more thought and patience to E.A.S.Y. than parents who fall somewhere in the middle. The descriptions below explain your score and outline the challenges you might face:

- **5 to 4**: You're probably a very organised person. You have a place for everything and like everything in its place. I'm sure you have no trouble with the idea of a structured routine – you even welcome it. You might find it difficult, though, to incorporate flexibility into your day and/or to make changes in your usual practices that factor in your baby's temperament and needs.

- **4 to 3**: You're fairly organised, although you tend not to be a fanatic about neatness or structure. Sometimes you let the house or your office space get a bit cluttered, but you eventually put things away, straighten up, file, or do whatever else is needed to restore order. You probably will have a relatively stress-free time putting your baby on E.A.S.Y. And because you seem to be somewhat flexible already, you won't have trouble adapting if your baby has other ideas.

- *3 to 2*: You tend to be a little scattered and disorganised, but you're far from a lost cause. To manage a structured routine, you may actually need to write down your routine so that you don't lose track. Note the exact times every day when your baby eats, plays and sleeps. You might also want to make lists of things you need to do. The good news for you is that you're already used to a little chaos, so life with baby might not be that much of a surprise.
- *2 to 1*: You're a real winger, a fly-by-the-seat-of-your-pants type. Managing a structured routine is going to be somewhat of a challenge. You definitely have to write everything down, which means a radical change in your lifestyle. But guess what? Having a baby *is* radical!

When E.A.S.Y. Seems Hard

It's rare, but some parents have a great deal of trouble establishing a structured routine. Usually it's for one of the following reasons:

- **They have no perspective**. In the greater scheme of things, infancy lasts but a moment. Parents who view E.A.S.Y. as a life sentence moan and groan and never get to understand or enjoy their baby.
- **They're not committed.** Your routine may change over time, or you may have to make adjustments because of your particular child or your own needs. Still, every day you must try to keep this structure pretty much as it is — eat, activity, sleep and time for yourself. It's a bit boring, but it works.
- **They can't take a practical middle road**. Either they believe in making baby conform to their needs, or they embrace an 'all-baby-all-the-time' philosophy in which baby (and chaos) rule the household.

How E.A.S.Y. Is Your Baby?

Naturally, how well a baby does also depends on the baby. What can you expect from your child? There's no way of knowing for sure. But I am certain of one thing: I have never encountered a baby who doesn't thrive on E.A.S.Y. nor a household that isn't improved by a structured routine. If you have an Angel baby or a Textbook baby, his inner clock will probably get him off to a good start without your doing much. But the other types of babies may need a bit more help. Here's what you might expect from your baby:

Angel
Not surprisingly, a baby with a mild, amenable disposition easily adapts to a structured day.

Textbook
Here is also a baby you can mould easily, because he's so predictable. Once you initiate a routine, he'll follow it without much diversion.

Touchy
This is our most fragile baby, who loves the predictability of a routine. The more consistent you are, the better you'll understand each other and the sooner she'll sleep through the night – usually by eight to 10 weeks if her cues are read correctly. But watch out if they aren't. Unless a Touchy baby is on a structured routine, it's hard to gauge her cries – and that will only make her more irritable.

Spirited

This baby, who has a mind of his own, may seem to resist your schedule. Or just when you think you have him on a good routine, he decides it's not working for him. You then have to take a day and watch his cues. See what he's asking you and then get him back on track. Spirited babies show you what works for them and what doesn't. It takes a Spirited baby about 12 weeks to start sleeping through the night. They act as though they don't want to stay asleep for fear of missing something. They also often have a hard time winding down.

Grumpy

Here is a baby who may not like any kind of routine, because she's disagreeable about most things. But if you can get her on track and be consistent about it, she'll be a lot happier. This type of baby is very intense, but you're less likely on E.A.S.Y. to have problems with bathing, dressing and even feeding, because at least your ornery little one will know what to expect – and will probably also be more content. A Grumpy often gets diagnosed as having colic when in actual fact all she needs is structure and perseverance. Grumpy babies often sleep through the night by six weeks. In fact, they seem happiest when they're tucked in bed, away from the bustle of the household.

Let me remind you, as I did when I first introduced these 'types' in Chapter 1: *your baby may exhibit the characteristics of more than one type*. In any case, you mustn't view these descriptions as if they're written in stone. However, I've found that some babies follow the E.A.S.Y. routine more easily than others. And some need a structured routine more than others.

But How Do I Learn What My Baby Needs?

Okay, so now you understand yourself and you have an idea of what to expect from your baby. The first few weeks on a structured routine may be rocky. It takes time and patience. And it takes the perseverance to stick with your plan. Here are some other tips to remember.

Write it all down
One of the tools I give parents, which is particularly helpful to wingers, is my E.A.S.Y. log (overleaf). It helps them keep track both of where they are in the process and what baby and Mum are doing. It's especially important to keep a log during the first six weeks of your baby's life. Remember to chart your own recovery as well.

This is only a sample log, designed primarily for mums. You might need to add another column indicating any special care that is needed. The important thing to remember is consistency – the log simply helps you keep track.

Your E.A.S.Y. Log

DATE

Eat						Activity		Sleep	You
AT WHAT TIME?	HOW MUCH (ML/OZ)?	ON RIGHT BREAST (MINUTES)?	ON LEFT BREAST (MINUTES)?	B O W E L M O V E M E N T	U R I N A T I O N	WHAT AND HOW LONG?	BATH (A.M. OR P.M.)?	HOW LONG?	REST? ERRANDS? INSIGHTS? COMMENTS?

Get to know your baby as a person

The challenge for you is to get to know your baby as the unique and special individual that she is. If your baby is named Rachel, don't think of her as 'the baby' – rather, think of her as a person named Rachel. You know the order in which Rachel's day should proceed – feeds,

> Remember that your baby is not really 'yours', but a separate person – a gift that you've been given to take care of.

activities, naps. But you also have to get Rachel's input. That may mean a few days of experimenting, holding back to watch what she's doing.

Take it easy…

Literally. E.A.S.Y. – the acronym – is also meant to be a reminder that babies respond to sweet, simple, slow movements. That's their natural rhythm, and we need to be respectful of it. Instead of trying to get your baby to respond to your pace, slow yourself down to hers. That way, you'll be able to look and listen, instead of rushing in. Besides being good for her, it's good for you to match the rhythm of her less stressful tempo. That's why I suggest taking three deep breaths before you even pick up your baby.

CHAPTER FIVE
The E – Eating

Breast or Bottle?

As a new mum it is difficult to decide whether to breastfeed your baby or to use bottles. My advice is to try to maintain a balanced view and, in the end, decide what's right for you. Take all opinions into account, but be cautious about whom and what you consult; know what a particular resource is trying to 'sell'. As for friends, listen to their experiences, but pay less attention to the horror stories.

- Explore the differences between formula-feeding and breastfeeding.

- Consider logistics and your own lifestyle.

- Know yourself – your level of patience, your comfort with the idea of nursing in public, your feelings about your breasts and nipples, and any preconceived notions of motherhood that might affect your view.

- Remember that you can change your mind and that you can always decide to do both.

Making the choice
Here are a few points to consider when deciding whether to breastfeed or bottle-feed:

- *Mother/child bonding*. Breastfeeding advocates go on about 'bonding' as a reason for women to breastfeed. I grant you that women feel a special closeness when a baby suckles, but mums who formula-feed also feel close to their infants. Besides, I don't think that's what cements the relationship between mother and child. True closeness comes when you get to know who your baby is.

- *Baby's health*. Many studies trumpet the benefits of breast milk, and breastfeeding advocates typically list a whole range of particular illnesses that mother's milk can prevent, including ear infections, strep throat, gastrointestinal problems, and upper respiratory diseases. It is, however, important to remember that formula today is more refined and chock-full of nutrients than ever. While it may not offer an infant natural immunity, formula definitely provides babies with all the nutrients they need to thrive. In the UK all infant formula milk must meet certain government-regulated standards in terms of composition and these have been set out in the 1995 Infant and Follow-on Formula Regulations.

- *Mother's postpartum recovery*. After delivery, breastfeeding offers several benefits to mums. The hormone that's released – oxytocin – speeds delivery of the placenta and constricts uterine blood vessels, which minimises blood loss. As the mother continues to nurse, repeated release of this hormone causes the uterus to return more quickly to its pre-pregnancy size. Another plus is quicker weight loss after delivery; the internal production of milk burns calories. This is offset, however, by the fact that a nursing mum needs to keep extra weight to ensure that the baby is getting proper nutrition. With formula, there are no such concerns. No matter how a mum feeds, her breasts may be sore and sensitive. A formula-feeder has to go through a sometimes painful period as the milk in her breasts dries up, but a breastfeeding mum might have other breast problems.

- *Mother's long-term health*. Studies suggest, but do not prove, that breastfeeding might offer women protection against pre-menopausal breast cancer, osteoporosis and ovarian cancer.

- *Mother's body image*. After the baby arrives, women often say, 'I want my body back.' It's not just a matter of losing weight. It's more about body image.

Breastfeeding feels to some women as if they have to 'give up' their bodies. Also, breastfeeding does change the look of most women's breasts even more than pregnancy does.

• *Difficulty*. Although breastfeeding, by definition, is 'natural', the technique is nonetheless a learned skill – more difficult, at least initially, than feeding a baby formula through a bottle. It's important for mothers to practise the art of breastfeeding, even before the baby arrives.

• *Convenience*. We hear much about the convenience of breastfeeding. In part, it's true, especially in the middle of the night. However, most women also pump breast milk, which means they have to take the time to express their milk, and they have to deal with bottles as well. Finally, breast milk is always the right temperature. But here's something you may not know: formula doesn't need to be warmed (babies don't seem to show a preference), so, at least in the premixed version, it's almost as convenient as breast milk. Both require storage precautions as well.

• *Cost*. Breastfeeding is definitely the less costly alternative, because breast milk is free. Even if you factor in the cost of a breastfeeding consultant, classes, various accessories and rental of a breast pump for a year, the monthly toll is around half the average monthly outlay if you buy formula.

• *Your partner's role*. Some fathers feel left out when a mum breastfeeds, but this must be a woman's choice. But a partner can participate whether mum decides to give the baby formula or breast milk, as long as she's willing to pump her milk. With either feeding regime, a father's help translates into a much-needed breather for the mother.

A word to Dad

You may want your wife to breastfeed because your mother or sister did, or because you think it's best. Or you may not want her to. Either way, your wife is an individual; she has choices in life, and this is one of them. She doesn't love you any the less if she wants to breastfeed; she's not a bad mum if she doesn't. I'm not saying you both shouldn't discuss your concerns, but ultimately, this is her decision to make.

- *Contra-indications for baby*. Based on the results of metabolic screening, which is routinely done on newborns to test for a number of different diseases, your paediatrician may advise against breastfeeding. In fact, in some cases very specific lactose-free formulas are indicated. Likewise, if a baby has a high degree of jaundice (caused by an excess of bilirubin, a yellowish substance usually broken down by the liver), some hospitals will insist on formula. As for allergies to formula, I think some people tend to be overly concerned about this. A mum will tell me that her baby got a rash or wind from a particular formula, but breastfed babies develop these problems, too.

- *Contra-indications for the mother*. Some mothers can't breastfeed, either because they've had surgery on their breasts, because they have an infection, such as HIV, or because they're taking a drug that taints their milk, such as lithium or any major tranquilliser. The bottom line is that while it is good for a baby to have some breast milk, especially during the first month, if that's not the mother's choice, or if for some reason the mother can't breastfeed, formula-feeding is a perfectly acceptable alternative – for some, the preferable alternative.

- *Feeding fashions*. Today, breastfeeding is all the rage. That doesn't mean formula is 'bad'. In the post-war decades, in fact, the majority believed that formula was best for babies, and only a third of all mothers nursed their babies. In 2005, 76 per cent of mums in Great Britain and Northern Ireland breastfed initially, although this figure drops considerably by the time the baby reaches six months of age. (Data from the NHS Information Centre's 2005 Infant Feeding Survey.)

Eating Profiles

Temperament influences the way a baby eats. Predictably, Angel and Textbook babies are usually good feeders, but so are Spirited babies. Touchy babies often get frustrated, especially if they're breast-fed. These infants don't allow for much flexibility. If you start to feed a Touchy baby in one position, he needs to feed that way all the time. You also can't talk loud while you're feeding him, change your position, or move to another room. Grumpy babies are impatient. If you are breastfeeding, they don't like to wait for the letdown. They sometimes tug on Mum's breast. They're often fine with a bottle, as long as it has a free-flowing nipple.

Feeding Happily Ever After

Starting in the right way is half the battle.

- Set aside a special place in your home – your baby's nursery or some quiet spot away from the hubbub of the household – and reserve that space solely for feeds.

- Take your time.

- Respect your baby's right to have a peaceful meal. Don't be on the telephone or having a chat across the fence with your neighbour, baby in hand. Feeding is an interactive process; you must pay attention, too. It's how you get to know your baby. And it's how your baby gets to know you. Also, as your baby becomes older, he or she will be more susceptible to visual and auditory distractions, which can disrupt his meal.

Feeding positions

Whether you feed by breast or bottle, you should nestle your baby comfortably in the crook of your arm, pretty much level with your breast (even if you're bottle-feeding), so that his head is elevated slightly, his body is in a straight line, and he doesn't have to strain his neck in order to attach to your breast or take his bottle. His inner arm is tucked down, next to him or around your side. Take care not to tilt him so that his head is lower than his body, as that will make it difficult for him to swallow. If you're bottle-feeding, your baby should be lying on his back; if breastfeeding, he should be turned slightly towards you, his face on to your nipple.

Hiccups

All babies get hiccups, sometimes after feeding, sometimes after a nap. They're thought to be caused by a full tummy or eating fast, which is exactly what happens to adults who bolt down their food. The diaphragm gets out of rhythm. There is not much you can do – except bear in mind that hiccups go as quickly as they start.

Burping

Whether they are breastfed or bottle-fed, all babies swallow air. I like to burp babies before we give the breast or bottle, because babies swallow air even when they're lying down, and then burp them again when they're finished. Or if a baby stops in the middle of a feed and starts fussing, that often means she has a little air. In that case, a mid-feed burp would be appropriate.

There are two ways to burp a baby. One is to sit your baby upright on your lap and gently rub her back while resting her chin on your hand. The other way, which I personally prefer, is to hold the baby upright with her arms relaxed and flopped over your shoulder. Her legs should be straight down, creating a direct route for the air to move up and out. Gently rub in an upward motion on the left-hand side at the level of her tummy. (If you pat her any lower, you're patting the kidneys.) With some babies a rub is all you need; others need gentle patting as well.

If you have been patting and rubbing for five minutes and there is no burp, you can pretty much assume that your baby doesn't have any air bubbles in his tummy. If you lay him down and he starts to squirm, gently pick him up – and out will come a luscious burp.

Intake and weight gain

No matter how they feed, new mums often worry, 'Is my baby eating enough?' Formula-feeding mums can see what their infants ingest. However, one clear indicator that your baby is feeding well is that your newborn will have six to nine wet nappies in a 24-hour period. The urine will be pale yellow to almost clear in colour. He will also have two to five bowel movements, which will vary from yellow to tan with a mustard-like consistency.

If you use disposable nappies, they will absorb the urine so well that it's hard to tell when your baby pees or what colour it is. During the first 10 days especially, place a tissue in your baby's nappy to determine if he is urinating and how often.

Finally, the best indicator of intake is weight gain, although it is important to remember that normal newborns lose up to 10 per cent of their birth weight in the first few days. Most full-term babies will return to their birth weight in seven to 10 days, at most two weeks. However, babies under 2.75kg (6lb) can't afford to lose 10 per cent of their weight. In such cases, supplement with formula until the breast milk comes in.

The normal range of weight gain is between 115–200g (4–7oz) a week. But before you start obsessing about your baby's weight gain, bear in mind that breastfed infants tend to be leaner and gain weight slightly more slowly than their bottle-fed counterparts.

Falling asleep while feeding

When your baby dozes off during a feed, try any of these strategies to jump-start his sucking reflex:

- with your thumb, gently rub in a circular motion the palm of his hand

- rub his back or underarm

- 'walk' your fingers up and down his spine – a technique I call 'walking the plank'

If none of these strategies works, I would leave him for half an hour and just let him sleep. If your baby constantly falls asleep while feeding and it's difficult to rouse him, ask your midwife's or health visitor's advice.

The Breastfeeding Basics

As when you learn any skill, the keys are patience and practice. Read, attend an antenatal class, or join a breastfeeding support group. Here, in my view, are some of the most important aspects of breastfeeding.

Latching on

The major (and often only) cause of breastfeeding problems is improper latch-on. You can understand about proper latch-on while still pregnant by placing two little round plasters on your breasts, 25mm (1in) above and below the nipple, which is precisely where you'll be holding your breasts when nursing. This gets you used to placing your fingers properly. Try it yourself – and practise. Remember that babies do not manually suck milk from the nipple; milk is produced through the stimulation the baby's sucking provides.

For a proper latch-on, your baby's lips should be flanged around the nipple and areola. As for correct positioning, extend his neck slightly, so that his nose and chin touch your breast. This will help keep his nose clear without your having to hold your breast. If you're large-breasted, put a sock under your breast to keep it up.

First feeds

Do the first feed as close to your baby's birth as you can. The first feed is important – but not for the reason you may think. Your baby isn't necessarily hungry. However, the first feed establishes a blueprint in his memory of how to latch on correctly. For the first two or three days, you'll produce colostrum – the 'power bar' component of breast milk. It's thick and yellow, more like honey than milk, and it's packed full of protein. During this time, when your breast milk is almost pure colostrum, you'll nurse 15 minutes on one side, 15 on the other. When you begin to produce breast milk, however, you'll switch to single-side feeding.

What's in breast milk?
If you left a bottle of breast milk out for an hour, it would separate into three parts. From top to bottom, you would see a progressively thicker liquid, which is also what your milk is like as it's delivered to your baby:

1. *Quencher* (first 5–10 minutes). This is more like skimmed milk – I think of it as the soup course, because it satisfies baby's thirst. It's rich in oxytocin, the same hormone released during lovemaking, which affects both mother and child. Mum gets really relaxed, similar to the feeling after an orgasm, and baby gets sleepy. This part of breast milk also has the highest concentration of lactose.

2. *Foremilk* (starts 5–8 minutes into the feed). More like the consistency of regular milk, foremilk has a high protein content, which is good for bones and brain development.

3. *Hind milk* (starts 15–18 minutes into the feed). This is thick and creamy, and it's where all the goody-goody fat is – the 'dessert' that helps your baby put on weight.

In the morning, after a good night's rest, your breast milk is richest in fat. If your baby seems extra-hungry at night, pump early in the day and save that fat-rich milk for a night-time feed. This will give your baby the extra calories she needs, allow you and hubby an evening break, and, most importantly, silence that ever-annoying voice that says, 'Am I producing enough milk to sustain my baby?'

Breastfeeding: the First Four Days

When babies are 2.75kg (6lb) or more at birth, I usually give their mums a chart like this to guide them through the first few feeds.

	Left Breast	**Right Breast**
First day: feed all day, whenever baby wants	5 minutes	5 minutes
Second day: feed every 2 hours	10 minutes	10 minutes
Third day: feed every 2½ hours	15 minutes	15 minutes
Fourth day: begin single-side feeding and your E.A.S.Y. routine	40 minutes maximum, every 2½–3 hours, switching breast each feed	

After breastfeeding, always wipe your nipples with a clean washcloth. The residue of milk can be a breeding ground for bacteria and cause thrush on your breast and in your baby's mouth. Never use soap, because it dries out your nipples.

Know your own breast milk and how your breasts produce it

Taste it. That way, if it has been stored, you'll know whether or not it has soured. Some mums have a fast letdown, as the milk ejection reflex is known, which means that their milk flow is quite rapid. Their babies sometimes tend to sputter and choke in the first few minutes of a feed. To stop fast letdown, put a finger on the nipple, as if you're stopping a flow of blood from a cut. When mothers have a slow milk ejection reflex, their babies appear frustrated and may pop on and off the breast to try to stimulate the flow. Slow letdown may be a sign of tension; try to relax more, perhaps by listening to a meditation tape before a feed. If that doesn't work, 'prime' your breasts with a hand pump until you see the milk flow, and then put the baby on your breast. It can take three minutes for this to happen, but it saves the baby from becoming frustrated.

> After every feed, put a safety pin in your bra to mark the breast you'll use next. You might also feel a fullness in the breast that hasn't been emptied.

Don't switch sides
If you switch sides after the first 10 minutes, at best your baby is only starting to get foremilk and never gets to the hind milk.

Don't watch the clock
Breastfeeding is never about time or quantity. It's about becoming aware of yourself and your baby. Breastfed babies usually feed a bit more frequently because breast milk is digested more quickly than formula. So if you have a two- or three-month-old infant nursing for 40 minutes, his system will have digested the entire amount within three hours. (See below for guidelines about how long it might take for your baby to feed.)

But how much?
Unless you pump and weigh your milk (see tip below on 'yielding'), it's hard to know the amount your baby's getting. Although I don't advise watching the clock, many mums ask the approximate time it takes a baby to nurse. As babies grow, they become more efficient

eaters and take less time. Below is an estimate, followed by the approximate amounts consumed at each feed:

4–8 weeks
Up to 40 minutes
60–150ml (2–5oz)

8–12 weeks
Up to 30 minutes
120–180ml (4–6oz)

3–6 months
Up to 20 minutes
150–240ml (5–8oz)

If you're worried about your supply of breast milk, do what I call a 'yield' for two or three days. It's a concept taken from my farming roots. Once a day, 15 minutes before a feed, pump your breasts and measure what you are yielding. Taking into account that a baby can extract at least 30ml (1oz) more by physically sucking at your breast, you have a good idea of what you're producing.

Storing breast milk
Breast milk can be stored in sterilised bottles or specially designed plastic bags meant to hold it (chemicals from ordinary plastic bags can leach into the milk). Either way, it should always be labelled with the date and time. Store milk in 60ml and 120ml (2oz and 4oz) containers to avoid waste.

Freshly expressed breast milk cannot be stored at room temperature. It should be placed in the fridge immediately, but not stored for longer than 48 hours.

It can be stored in the freezer for up to six months, but it's not advisable because the composition of breast milk changes as your baby grows. Therefore store no more than a dozen 120ml (4oz) bags and rotate them every four weeks using the oldest ones first.

Remember that breast milk is human fluid. Always wash your hands, and keep handling to a minimum. If possible, pump directly into freezer bags.

Thaw breast milk by placing the sealed container in a bowl of warm water for around 30 minutes. Never use a microwave; it will change the composition of your milk by breaking down the protein. Gently swirl the container to blend any fat that may have separated and risen during thawing. Feed thawed milk immediately or store it in the fridge for no longer than 24 hours. You can combine fresh breast milk with thawed, but never refreeze.

Find a mentor

There's no one better to help you over the initial hurdles than another woman who's recently been through it. If there's no one to turn to, talk to the midwife or health visitor in your area who can arm you with preventive measures and be on call should any problems develop. Pick your mentor wisely – someone who has patience, a sense of humour, and good feelings about breastfeeding. Take negative input or far-fetched stories with a pinch of salt. This brings to mind poor Gretchen, who told me she didn't want to breastfeed 'because my friend's baby swallowed her nipple'!

Watch your diet

Throughout the day, the calories you ingest are for your baby, as well as for your own body. That's why it's so important to sustain your intake of food while breastfeeding – no crash diets. Maintain a healthy, well-balanced diet, high in protein and complex carbohydrates. Also, because your baby is taking fluid from your body, too, be sure to drink 16 glasses of water per day – twice the recommended amount.

Be flexible

Though I recommend a structured feeding routine, I'm not saying that if a baby lets forth a hunger cry after two hours, you don't feed him. In fact, during a growth spurt, he or she may need to eat a bit more often. What I am saying is that your baby will eat better and his intestines will work better if he gets proper meals at regular intervals.

Expressing milk

Pumping or expressing breast milk is not meant to replace breastfeeding, but rather to complement and enhance the experience. It allows you to empty your breasts so that your baby can have your breast milk even when you're not around to give it to her. It can also prevent problems such as engorgement (see page 71). Make sure a midwife or lactation consultant shows you how to use the pump properly.

What type of pump?

If your baby is premature, you'll need a strong industrial type. If you plan to be away from your baby only occasionally, a hand or foot pump will do. Buy or rent a pump in which the motor can be regulated for speed and strength. Stay away from those that require you to adjust the pump cycle manually by placing your finger over a hose – they're unsafe.

Should I buy or rent?
Buy if you're returning to work and plan to breastfeed for a year; rent if you plan to breastfeed for less than six months. Rented pumps are always serviced and, therefore, can be shared, as long as each person purchases new attachments. Pumps you buy are best used by one person.

When should I express?
Generally, it takes an hour after a feed for your milk to replenish itself. To increase your supply, for two days express 10 minutes after the baby has fed. On returning to work, if you can't pump at the time you'd normally feed, at least do it at the same time every day – for example, 15 minutes at lunchtime.

Where can I express?
Don't express in the loo at work; it's unsanitary. Close the door to your office or find some other quiet place. One of my mums told me that on her job they had a 'pump room', which was kept scrupulously clean for breastfeeding mothers.

Keep a breastfeeding diary
Once you get past the first few days and begin single-side feeding, I always suggest keeping track of when your baby feeds, for how long, on which breast, and other pertinent details. Below, I've reprinted the sheet I give out to my mums. Feel free to adapt it to suit your needs. You'll see that I filled in examples on the first two lines.

Time of day	Which breast?	Duration of feed	Do you hear swallowing?	Number of wet nappies since last feed	Number and colour of stools since last feed	Supple-ment: water or formula?	Amount of milk pumped	Other
6 A.M.	☒ L ☐ R	35 min.	☒ Y ☐ N	1	1 yellow very soft	none	1 oz. @ 7.15 A.M.	Seemed a little fussy after eating
8.15 A.M.	☒ L ☐ R	30 min.	☒ Y ☐ N	1	0	none	1.5 oz. @ 8.30 A.M.	Had to wake him during the feed
	☐ L ☐ R		☐ Y ☐ N					
	☐ L ☐ R		☐ Y ☐ N					
	☐ L ☐ R		☐ Y ☐ N					
	☐ L ☐ R		☐ Y ☐ N					
	☐ L ☐ R		☐ Y ☐ N					
	☐ L ☐ R		☐ Y ☐ N					
	☐ L ☐ R		☐ Y ☐ N					

Observe my 40-day rule

Some women get the hang of breastfeeding within a few days; some take longer. If you're one of the latter, please don't start panicking. Give yourself 40 days of not expecting too much. For some women, it will take that long to get into breastfeeding. Even with a proper latch-on, you may experience a problem in your breasts (see below), or your baby may not catch on at once. Allow time for trial and error.

Breastfeeding Trouble-shooting Guide

Engorgement
Breasts become filled with fluid. Sometimes this is milk, but more often it's the surplus fluid – blood, lymph fluid and water – that settles in the extremities, especially after a C-section.

- *Symptoms*: Breasts are hard, hot, swollen; may be accompanied by flu-like symptoms – fever, chills, night sweats; can also make it difficult for baby to latch on, thereby causing sore nipples.

- *What to do*: Wrap breasts in a hot, wet cloth nappy; do over-arm exercise (ball-throwing motion), five sets every two hours, just before you feed, and rotate your arms and ankles. Consult a doctor if the condition has not lessened within 24 hours.

Blocked milk duct
Milk congeals in lactiferous duct and becomes the consistency of cottage cheese.

- *Symptoms*: Localised lump in breast, painful to the touch.

- *What to do*: If untreated, this can lead to mastitis. Apply heat and rub your breasts in a small circular motion around the lump, stroking towards the nipple. Imagine yourself trying to knead a curd of cottage cheese in order to turn it into milk. (You won't actually see the milk come out of your breast.)

Pain in nipples

- *Symptoms:* Nipples may be cracked, sore, tender, and/or red; chronic cases evidence blisters, burning, bleeding, and pain throughout and between feedings.

- *What to do:* A normal condition for the first few days of nursing, which will disappear once your baby begins rhythmic sucking. If the discomfort persists, your baby is not latched on correctly. Seek the help of a lactation consultant.

Oxytocin overload

- *Symptoms:* Mum gets sleepy during breastfeeding because of the production of 'love hormone' – the same hormone released during orgasm.

- *What to do*: No real prevention, but it might be a good idea to try to get more rest between feedings.

Headache

- *Symptoms:* Occurs during or immediately after feeding, the result of your pituitary gland releasing oxytocin and prolactin.

- *What to do:* Seek medical advice if it persists.

Rash

- *Symptoms:* All over the body, like hives.

- *What to do:* An allergic reaction to oxytocin. Antihistamines are usually recommended, but talk to your doctor first.

Yeast infection

- *Symptoms:* Breasts are sore, or you feel a burning sensation in them; your baby may also have a nappy rash with red spots.

- **What to do:** Call your doctor. You might both need medication to take care of the infection; your baby will need cream or ointment for his bottom, but don't use it on your breasts – it can clog your glands.

Mastitis
Inflammation of the mammary gland.

- **Symptoms:** Uneven bright red line across the breasts; breasts are hot; flu-like symptoms as well.

- **What to do:** Consult a doctor immediately.

Breastfeeding Bugaboos

'My baby often squirms halfway through his feed'

- **Why?** In infants under four months, this could mean that she needs to have a bowel movement. She can't poo and suck at the same time.

- **What to do:** Take her off the breast, lay her on your lap, allow her to poo, and then resume nursing.

'My baby often falls asleep when I'm trying to feed him'

- **Why?** Your baby may be getting a heavy dose of oxytocin. Or he might be snacking and really isn't hungry.

- **What to do**: To wake a sleeping baby, see the tip on page 61. But also ask yourself: 'Is my baby on a structured routine?' This is the best way to determine whether he's really hungry. If he's eating every hour, he may be snacking instead of getting a good bellyful of food. Put him on E.A.S.Y.

'My baby bobs on and off my breast'

- **Why**? It could be impatience with a slow letdown. If it's accompanied by her pulling her legs up, it could be gas. Or she might not be hungry.

- **What to do**: If this happens repeatedly, you probably have a slow letdown reflex. 'Prime' yourself by pumping first. If it's gas, try the remedies on page 59. If none of these works, she's probably not interested in nursing. Take her off your breast.

'My baby seems to "forget" how to latch on'

- **Why**? All babies, especially boys, at times 'forget' – they lose focus. It also can mean that a baby is over-hungry.

- **What to do**: Put your pinky into your baby's mouth for a few seconds, to give him a focus and a reminder of how to suck. Then pop him back on the breast. If he's over-hungry and you know you have slow letdown, prime your breasts before latching him on.

Formula-feeding Basics

It doesn't matter what your reasons are; if you've read, researched and come to the conclusion that you want to put your baby on formula, that's fine. Stand up for your right to give your baby formula.

Don't compare your feeding regime to a breastfeeding mother's. Formula is digested more slowly than human milk, which means that formula-fed babies can often go four hours between feeds, instead of three.

Choosing a formula

Read the ingredients. There are lots of different types of formulas out there, all of which must adhere to the 1995 Infant and Follow-on Formula Regulations. Basically, formula is made with either cow's milk or soy. Personally, I prefer cow-based formulas to soy-based, although both are fortified with vitamins, iron and other nutrients.

Storage

Formula, which comes in powdered form, concentrate or, for even greater convenience, ready-mixed, is dated by the manufacturer. Cans can be kept unopened until the last-use date. Once in bottles, however, no matter which formula you use, it only keeps 24 hours. Most manufacturers do not recommend freezing. As with breast milk, never use a microwave; though it doesn't change the composition of formula, it heats the liquid unevenly and can scald your baby. Never re-use a bottle that your baby hasn't finished. To avoid waste, prepare only 60ml and 120ml (2oz and 4oz) bottles until your newborn has demonstrated a bigger capacity.

Bottles and teats

For a newborn, the best type of teat is one that only allows the milk to come out when the infant sucks hard, just as they have to with breastfeeding. For example, the Avent Airflex teat has a built-in one-way air valve which means that the milk flows only at a pace that your baby controls. Until your baby is three or four weeks old, I would suggest that you do some research and invest in a good-quality feeding system, even if it may cost a bit more than other brands. Switch to a slow-flow teat for the second month, a second-stage teat for the third month, and a regular-flow teat from the fourth month until weaning.

When shopping for bottles and teats, also look for combinations that have a universal screw top, so that you can interchange if necessary. I've seen a few systems that are very pleasing to the eye and come with all sorts of fantastic promises – 'just like mother's breast', 'natural tilt', 'prevents wind', etc. Take the advertising with a pinch of salt, and see which works best for your baby.

Be gentle

The first time you put a teat into your baby's mouth, stroke her lips with the teat of the bottle and wait until she responds by opening her mouth. Then gently slide the teat in as she latches on. Never force a bottle into your baby's mouth.

How much formula?

With formula-feeding, the composition never changes, as it does with mother's milk, but as she grows, the baby understandably needs to eat more.

Birth to 3 weeks: 90ml (3oz) every 3 hours
3–6 weeks: 120ml (4oz) every 3 hours
6–12 weeks: 120–180ml (4–6oz) (usually plateauing at 180ml/6oz by 3 months) every 4 hours
3–6 months: increases to 240ml (8oz) every 4 hours

The Third Alternative: Breast and Bottle

My even-handedness about breast milk and formula aside, I always tell parents that even a little bit of breast milk is better than none. Some mums are shocked to hear this, especially those who have consulted doctors or organisations that advocate breastfeeding and believe that feeding is an all-or-nothing proposition.

'Can I really do both?' they ask. 'Is it possible to nurse my baby and give her a bottle?' My answer is always, 'Of course you can.' I also explain that by 'both' I mean that a baby can be given breast milk and formula, or given only breast milk, but by bottle as well as by breast.

The myth of nipple confusion

A lot has been made of 'nipple confusion' as a reason for not feeding babies with both breast and bottle. I believe that's a myth. What can confuse a baby is flow, and that can be easily remedied. An infant on the breast uses different tongue muscles than a bottle-fed one. Also, a breastfeeder can regulate the amount of milk he takes in by changing the way he sucks, but with a bottle, there's a constant flow controlled by gravity, not the baby. If a baby chokes on a bottle, it's best to use a teat which allows a baby to get milk only when he sucks hard – like the Avent Airflex system. It is also important to find a teat that closely matches your own nipple. There are many different types of teats on the market – flat, long, short, bulbous – with bottles to match.

Making the switch

Within the first three weeks, babies easily switch back and forth from breast to bottle. If you wait, though, you'll probably have a tougher time.

What do you do?

For two days, keep presenting bottle and no breast (or vice versa, if you're trying to get a bottle-fed baby on the breast). Remember that babies are always willing to go back to their original feeding mode. Whether your baby is used to breast or bottle, once it's in his memory, there's no such thing as his rejecting it.

Beware!

This is hard work. Your baby will feel frustrated and cry a lot. He's saying to you, 'What the dickens are you trying to put into my mouth?' He might even gulp and sputter as he feeds, particularly if he's making the switch to a bottle, because he doesn't know how to regulate the stream of liquid that pours out of a rubber nipple. Again, using a teat like the Avent Airflex system will eliminate this flow problem.

Breast Manners

At around four months, babies' hands start to wander. So start now to teach your baby what I call 'breast manners'. In each case, the trick is to be firm but gentle, reminding her of your boundaries. Also, try breastfeeding in a quiet environment, to cut down on distractions.

Fiddling
Hold his hand and gently take it away from your body or whatever he's touching. Say, 'Mummy doesn't like that.'

Distractions
The worst is when a baby gets distracted and tries to turn her head … with Mum's nipple still in her mouth. When that happens, take her off the breast and say, 'Mummy doesn't like that.'

Biting
When a baby's teeth come in, almost every mum gets bitten. It should only happen once, though. Don't be afraid to react appropriately, pulling away and saying, 'Ouch, that hurts. Don't bite Mummy.' That's usually enough, but if it doesn't stop him, remove him from your breast.

Shirt-pulling
Toddlers still nursing sometimes do this when they want a dummy. Simply say, 'Mummy doesn't want her shirt up. Don't pull on it.'

Wean, Baby, Wean!

Weaning has come to mean two different things. Contrary to a popular misconception, weaning doesn't mean going off breast milk. Rather, it refers to a natural progression common to all mammals: the transition from a liquid diet, be it mother's milk or formula, to solid foods.

Most paediatricians and the World Health Organization suggest waiting until your baby is six months old before starting to introduce solid foods. With the exception of very large babies – 7.5–10kg (17–22lb) at four months – or infants suffering from oesophageal reflux, the baby equivalent of heartburn, I agree. Weaning is quite simple, actually, if you follow the following important guidelines.

- Start with one solid food. I prefer pears because they're easy to digest, but if your paediatrician suggests another food, such as rice cereal, by all means follow that. Give the new food twice a day, morning and afternoon, for two weeks before introducing a second solid.

- Always introduce a new food in the morning. This gives you all day to see if your baby is having an adverse reaction to the food, such as a rash, vomiting or diarrhoea.

- Never mix foods together. That way there's no question about allergic reactions to a particular food.

- Never force or struggle with a baby who doesn't want to eat a particular food. Feeding should be a pleasant experience for the baby and the whole family.

Weaning: the First 12 Weeks

The following 12-week schedule is based on weaning a six-month-old child. You will do the morning feed as usual, breast or bottle, and serve 'breakfast' two hours later. 'Lunch' should be midday and 'dinner' late afternoon. Complete breakfast and dinner by finishing on the breast or bottle. Remember that every baby is different; ask your paediatrician what's right for yours.

Week	Breakfast	Lunch	Dinner	Comments
1 (6 months old)	Pear, 2 teaspoons	Bottle or breast	Pear, 2 teaspoons	
2	Pear, 2 teaspoons	Bottle or breast	Pear, 2 teaspoons	
3	Squash, 2 teaspoons	Bottle or breast	Pear, 2 teaspoons	
4	Sweet potato, 2 teaspoons	Squash, 2 teaspoons	Pear, 2 teaspoons	
5 (over 7 months old)	Oatmeal, 4 teaspoons	Squash, 4 teaspoons	Pear	Increase the amount to meet your growing baby's needs.
6	Oatmeal and pear, 4 teaspoons each	Squash, 8 teaspoons	Oatmeal and sweet potato, 4 teaspoons each	Now you can give more than one food at a meal.
7	Peach, 8 teaspoons	Oatmeal and squash, 4 teaspoons each	Oatmeal and pear, 4 teaspoons each	

Week	Breakfast	Lunch	Dinner	Comments
8 (8 months old)	Banana	From this point on, you can mix and match the above foods, introducing a new food each week as shown at the left, 8–12 teaspoons per meal.		
9	Carrots			
10	Peas			
11	Green beans	You can continue to mix and match foods, introducing a new food each week as shown, 8–12 teaspoons per meal		
12 (9 months old)	Apple			

CHAPTER SIX
The A – Activity

I encourage parents to think about any activity their baby does as an opportunity to foster security and, at the same time, independence.

Drawing a Circle of Respect

Whether you're lifting your baby out of the cot in the morning, bathing him, or playing peekaboo, it's vital that you remember that he is a separate person, deserving of your undivided attention and respect, but also capable of acting on his own. If you keep in mind the following basic principles you will easily and naturally maintain a circle of respect during every activity your baby does:

- Be with your baby. Make her the undivided object of your attention at that moment. This is bonding time, so focus. Don't be on the phone, worrying about getting the laundry done, or ruminating on a report that you have to complete.

- Delight your baby's senses, but avoid over-stimulation. Our culture encourages excesses and over-stimulation – and parents unwittingly contribute to the problem, because they don't realise how delicate their baby's senses are or how much infants actually take in (see page 86). I'm not suggesting that we stop singing to our children, playing music for them, showing them brightly coloured objects, or even buying toys for them, but less is more where babies are concerned.

- Take care to make your baby's environment interesting, pleasant and safe. You don't need money for this, just common sense.

- Foster your baby's independence. This may sound counter-intuitive – how can a baby be independent? But he can gain confidence to venture forth, explore and play independently. Therefore, when your baby is at play, it's always a good idea to observe more than interact.

- Remember to talk with, not at, your baby. Having a dialogue implies a two-way process: whenever your child is involved in an activity, you watch and listen and wait for his response. If he tries to involve you, of course, you jump in. If he 'asks' for a change of scene, definitely honour his request. Otherwise, let him explore.

- Engage and inspire, but always let your baby lead. Never place a baby in a position she can't get into (or out of) on her own. Don't give her toys that are outside of her 'learning triangle' (see page 87).

From the time your baby wakes up until you tuck him in for his night-time sleep, keep the above guidelines in mind. Remember that everyone, including your baby, deserves to have personal space. Below, as I take you through your baby's day, you'll see how each of these principles comes to bear.

The Three-alarm Wake-up System

Some babies wake up and amuse themselves and never get past what I call the 'first alert' – they're content to hang out in their cribs until someone comes to get them. Others go through all three alerts quickly, no matter how fast you react.

- *Alert 1*: a creaking or fussy sound, accompanied by fidgeting. It means, 'Hello? Is anyone there? Why aren't you coming in to get me?'

- *Alert 2*: a cough-like cry in the back of the throat that stops and starts. When they stop, they're listening for you. When you don't come, they mean, 'Hey, get in here!'

• *Alert 3*: an all-out cry, with arms and legs flailing. 'Come in now! I'm serious!'

Waking Your Baby

Be gentle, quiet and considerate when you greet your baby in the morning. However, do remember that no matter how you do this, your little love bucket has ideas of his own. Here's a summary of what you might expect from our various baby types:

• *Angel*. All smiles, coos and goo-goos, these babies seem eternally happy to be in their environment. Unless they're particularly hungry or their nappy is soaked through, they're content to play in their crib until someone comes in to get them. In other words, they rarely go past the first wake-up alert (see page 84).

• *Textbook*. If you don't catch these babies by Alert 1, they let you know they're up by making little crotchety Alert 2 noises that mean, 'Get in here.' If you go in, saying, 'I'm right here – I didn't go anywhere,' they're fine. If you don't show up, they sound Alert 3 loud and clear.

• *Touchy*. These little ones almost always wake up crying. Because they need reassurance, they often sound the three alerts of waking in rapid succession. Unable to tolerate being left in their cribs for more than five minutes, they're likely to have a meltdown if you don't get there by Alert 1 or 2.

• *Spirited*. These babies, who are very active, high-energy types, often skip the first stage of waking up and immediately sound Alert 2. They fuss and squirm, uttering little cough-cough kind of cries, and will end up wailing if no one shows up at that point.

- *Grumpy*. Because they don't like to be wet or uncomfortable, these babies also sound the three alerts rather quickly. You can forget about coaxing a morning smile out of them – you could stand on your head or do somersaults, but these little ones still won't crack a smile.

Too Much Stimulation

My cardinal rule is this: if your baby is going through what seems like an unsettled period and is crying a lot, put away anything that shakes, rattles, jiggles, wiggles, squeaks or vibrates. Try it for just three days and see if baby calms down. (Unless something else is wrong, she usually will.)

Of course we should play music and sing to our children. Of course we should show them brightly coloured objects and even buy toys for them. But when we do too much and present infants with too many choices, they become over-stimulated.

What affects your baby			
Hearing (auditory)	Talking Humming Singing Heartbeat Music	Touch (tactile)	Contact with skin, lips, hair Cuddling Massage Water Cotton balls/cloth
Sight (visual)	Black-and-white cards Striped material Mobile Faces The environment	Smell (olfactory)	Humans Cooking odours Perfume Spices
Taste (gustatory)	Milk Other foods	Movement (vestibular)	Rocking Carrying Swinging Riding (buggy, car)

Playing Within the Learning Triangle

To know what fits inside your child's learning triangle, consider his accomplishments to date – what he can do. If you stay within his learning triangle, your child will acquire knowledge naturally, at his own pace. And remember my ground rule: *when your baby has a toy, observe rather than jump in.*

Listed below are some of the things you might expect from your baby as he reaches various stages of development.

He mostly watches and listens

For approximately the first six to eight weeks, your baby is an auditory and visual creature, but he's becoming progressively more alert and aware of his surroundings.

- Even though his vision extends only 20–30cm (8–12in), he can see you and may even reward you with a smile or a coo. Take a moment to 'answer' him.

- When your baby is not spending time looking at your face, you may notice that he also has a particular fondness for staring at lines. To him, straight lines appear to be moving, because his retinas are not yet fixed. With a black marker, draw straight lines on a white index card. These give your baby a focal point, which is important because his vision is still blurry and two-dimensional.

- With newborns I advise keeping only one or two toys in his cot or moses basket. Rotate them when he stops looking at them.

- Be aware of the impact of colour: primary colours stimulate babies; pastel colours calm them down. At any given time of day, choose colours to have a desired effect – for example, don't put a red-and-black flash card into the crib if your baby is getting ready for a nap.

She gains control over her head and neck

Once your baby is able to turn her head, usually somewhere in the second month, and move it from side to side, perhaps even lift it a bit (usually by the third month), she also has better control over her eyes. You might catch her watching her own hand. Even some one-month-old babies can imitate facial expressions – if the adult sticks out his tongue, the baby does, too; if he opens his mouth, so does the baby.

- This is a good time to invest in a clip-on mobile that you can move from crib to playpen. Babies like to turn their heads (often to the right), so don't position it directly in her line of sight – nor should it be any farther away than 35cm (14in).

- At this point (around eight weeks), your baby is beginning to see in three dimensions. Her posture has straightened out, and she holds her hands open much of the time. She catches her own hands, mostly by accident.

- She can remember and predict more accurately what comes next. In fact, at two months, babies can recognise and remember someone from a previous day.

- Now you can upgrade your homemade flash cards by drawing wavy lines, circles and simple pictures, like a house or a smiley face.

- You can put a mirror in her crib; when she smiles, it smiles back at her. However, remember that although your baby loves to stare at things, when she's had enough, she doesn't yet have the mobility that would enable her to move away from an object that no longer interests her.

He reaches and grasps

Pretty much anything – including his own body parts – can fascinate a baby who is able to reach and grasp, which happens at around three or four months. And everything goes straight into his mouth.

- His favourite plaything is you, but this is also a good time for simple, responsive toys, such as rattles and other safe objects that generate noise or feel good to the touch, like a foam hair curler.

- Infants love to explore and are thrilled when they can cause a reaction. Just watch your little one when he shakes a rattle; his eyes go wide. Babies comprehend cause and effect now, so anything that makes a noise gives them a feeling of accomplishment.

- He also knows how to get your attention when he's had enough. He'll drop a toy, make a cough-like noise in the back of his throat, or let forth a cranky little cry.

She can roll

The ability to roll over on to one side, which happens anywhere from the end of the third month to the fifth month, is the beginning of a baby's mobility. Before you know it, your baby will be rolling both ways, and the fun continues.

- She will still love toys that make a noise, but you can also give her everyday household items, like a spoon. These simple objects will be the source of endless delight. Watch her with a plastic plate and you will see her turn it this way and that, push away, and grab it again.

- She also will love to play with little shapes: cubes, balls or triangles. Believe it or not, by mouthing them, she's figuring out what they are and can sense their differences.

He can sit up

Babies can't sit up until they've grown into their heads, usually around six months old; before that, they're top-heavy. When babies can sit up by themselves, they begin to develop depth perception. Now he also is able to transfer objects from one hand to the other; he can point and gesture as well. His curiosity will propel him to move towards things, but physically he's not quite there yet.

- Let him explore on his own. He has control over his head, arms and torso at this point but not his legs. So he may lean forward and lunge for something he wants, but end up on his chest because he's still a bit top-heavy. Don't hand him that toy right away. Stand back; offer your encouragement instead. It inspires confidence to say, 'Good job. You're nearly there.'

- Use your judgement, though. You're just giving him a bit of parental encouragement. After he's tried to reach it, you can hand him the toy.

- Give him simple playthings that reinforce an action, like a clown or a jack-in-the-box that pops up when he pushes the right button or lever. Toys such as this are best because babies love to see that they can make things happen.

- Remember that less is more, and that many of the things you'll want to buy your baby won't amuse him. It's not a matter of like or dislike – your baby simply won't understand all his toys.

She can move
When your baby really starts to crawl, usually between eight and 10 months, it's time to childproof your house if you haven't already, so that you can create ample opportunities for her to explore. For child-proofing basics see page 92.

- The best playthings are toys that encourage her to put things in and take things out. Of course, she will initially be more proficient at undoing – she'll take everything out but rarely put anything back. Eventually, by around 10 months to a year, she'll gain the dexterity to put things together and even to clean up her toys from the floor and put them in the toy box.

- She probably will be able to pick up small objects, too, because her fine motor skills are developing, which enables her to master a pincer-like grasp, using her thumb and index finger.

- She also likes rolling toys, ones that she can pull towards her. And she might also start to develop an attachment for a particular toy, like a stuffed animal or a blanket.

- Now when you play nursery rhymes, you can add movements, which your baby can imitate. Songs and rhythms teach children about language and coordination.

- At this point, a favourite game will be peekaboo, which teaches your baby object permanence. This is important, because once your baby learns the concept, she also will understand that if you go into the next room, you don't disappear, either. You can reinforce this by saying, 'I'll be right back.'

- Use a variety of household items as playthings, and be creative. A spoon and a plate or pot are great for banging. A colander makes a wonderful peekaboo shield.

As your baby expands her physical and mental repertoire, remember that she is an individual. Watch her; learn who she is from what she does, rather than trying to make her into what you want her to be. As long as she's safe, supported and loved, she will blossom into an amazing and unique little being. She will be in constant motion, learn new skills every day, and never fail to surprise you.

Make sure everything your baby plays with is washable, sturdy and has no sharp edges or strings that can come loose and be swallowed. An object is too small to play with if it can fit inside a cardboard toilet-paper roll; it could get stuck in baby's throat or pushed into an ear or nose.

Childproofing Basics

The trick is to look at your home from the eyes (and height) of a child. Get down on all fours and crawl around! Following are the dangers you'll want to prevent.

- *Poisoning*. Remove all cleaning fluids and other dangerous substances from under the kitchen and bathroom sinks and store them in high cabinets. Even if you install clips to lock cupboard doors, can you risk a strong or clever toddler breaking in? Purchase a first-aid kit. If you believe your baby has ingested a poisonous substance, call your doctor or 999 before doing anything.

- *Airborne pollutants*. Have your home checked for radon, a naturally emitted radioactive gas. Install smoke and carbon monoxide detectors – and check the batteries regularly. Stop smoking, and don't allow anyone else to smoke in your home or car.

- *Strangling*. Keep drape and blind cords, as well as electric wires, out of reach by using pegs or masking tape to secure them above baby level.

- *Electric shock*. Cover all outlets, and make sure every lamp socket in your house has a lightbulb in it.

- *Drowning*. Never leave your baby unattended in the bath. Install a cover lock on the toilet, too. Baby is still top-heavy and can fall into the bowl and drown.

- *Burns and scalding*. Install stove knob guards. Secure a cover over the bath tap, either with a plastic guard (available in most hardware stores) or by wrapping a towel around it, which prevents baby both from touching a hot tap and from sustaining a serious injury if she hits her head. Set your water heater to 49°C (120°F) to avoid scalding.

- *Falling and stair accidents*. Once your baby becomes active, if you still use a changing table, keep a hand and two eyes on him at all times. Install gates at the top and bottom of the stairs, but don't let yourself become complacent. Always be right next to him when your baby is beginning to learn how to climb stairs. He'll be an ace at going up, but he won't know how to get down.

- *Cot accidents*. Always buy or use a cot that is guaranteed to be built to British Standard EN 716. If you have an old or antique cot or crib, make sure that the slats are not wider apart than BS EN 716 specifies. Cot bumpers, an American invention, were a shock to me when I first went to America. I usually tell parents to put them away, because active babies can roll under them and get stuck or, worse, suffocate.

It only takes a few days to teach a child not to touch something, but you will probably have to repeat the process in different areas of the house, with various objects. During this teaching phase replace your most valuable and treasured ornaments with inexpensive articles.

CHAPTER SEVEN
The S – Sleep

Good Sleep, Good Baby

In their earliest days, babies sleep more than they do any other single thing – some as much as 23 hours a day during the first week! When an infant sleeps, his brain is busy manufacturing new brain cells, which are needed for mental, physical and emotional development.

The most important thing every new parent should understand is that babies need their parents' direction to establish proper sleep habits. In fact, the reason so-called sleep problems are common is because so many parents don't realise that they, not their babies, must control bedtime.

What Is Sensible Sleep?

In my view, babies need to learn how to fall asleep on their own; they need to feel safe and secure in their own cots. But they also need us to comfort them when they're distressed. The first set of goals won't be met unless we also bear in mind the second. At the same time, parents need to have adequate rest, moments for themselves and each other, and a life that isn't all-baby-all-the-time.

Start as you mean to go on

If you're initially attracted to the notion of 'shared sleeping', think it through. Is this how you want it to be three months from now? Six months? Longer? Remember that everything you do teaches your baby. Therefore, when you put him to bed by cuddling him on your chest or rocking him for 40 minutes, in effect you're instructing him. You're saying, 'This is how you get to sleep.' Once you go down that road, then you'd better be prepared to cuddle and rock him for a long, long time.

Observe without intervention

You may recall this directive when I talked about playing with your baby in Chapter 6 'The A – Activity' and also in Chapter 3 'Understanding Your Baby'. The same holds true for sleeping. Babies go through a predictable cycle each time they fall asleep. Parents need to understand this so that they don't rush in. Rather than interrupting a baby's natural flow, we need to step back and let the baby fall asleep on his own.

Don't make your baby dependent on props

A prop is any device or intervention that when withdrawn will cause an infant distress. We can't expect babies to learn how to fall asleep on their own if we train them to believe that Dad's chest, a 30-minute carry, or a breast in the mouth will always be there to soothe them. As I point out on page 101, I'm all for dummies, but not when they're used to 'dummy up'. Of course, if your child is comforted by a favourite cuddly toy, allow her to have it. But I'm against anything you give to quieten her. Instead, let her discover her own means of calming herself.

Develop bedtime and naptime rituals

Bedtimes and naptimes must be done the same way each time. As I've stressed throughout, babies are creatures of habit. They like to know what's coming next, and research has proven that even very young infants who have been conditioned to expect a particular stimulus are able to predict when it's coming.

Know how your particular baby goes to sleep

The best way is to keep a sleep diary. Starting in the morning, write down baby's wake-up time and keep track of every nap during the day. Note when he goes to bed and when he wakes in the middle of the night. Do this for four days, which is a long enough period to give you an indication of your baby's sleep patterns, even if his naptimes seem erratic.

Sleep Types

Although there is a predictable three-stage process to falling asleep (see below), it's important to know how your baby drifts off. If the cycle is not interrupted by an adult's intervention, Angel and Textbook babies will fall asleep easily and independently. With a Touchy baby, who is prone to meltdowns, you have to be ultra-observant; if you miss this baby's window, he gets keyed up and it's very hard for him to wind down. A Spirited baby tends to fidget a lot; you may have to block out her visual stimulation. She sometimes gets a wild, wide-eyed look when she's tired, as if there are little matchsticks propping her eyelids open. A Grumpy baby may fuss a little, but he's usually happy to have his nap.

The Three Stages of Sleep

Babies pass through these stages every time they fall asleep. The entire process usually takes around 20 minutes.

Stage 1: The Window
Your baby can't say 'I'm tired', but he will show you by yawning and exhibiting other signs of fatigue (see page 99). By the third yawn, get him to bed. If you don't, he'll start to cry rather than pass into the next stage.

Stage 2: The Zone
At this point, your baby has a fixed, focused gaze – or, as I call it, the 'seven-mile stare' – that lasts for three or four minutes. His eyes are open, but he's not really seeing – he's off somewhere in the stratosphere.

Stage 3: Letting Go
Now your baby resembles a person nodding off on a train. He closes his eyes and his head drops forward or to the side. Just as he seems to be falling asleep, his eyes open suddenly and his head whips backwards, jolting his whole body. He'll then close his eyes again and repeat the process anywhere from three to five times more until he finally enters dreamland.

Baby Sleep

When they're asleep, babies, like adults, progress through cycles of sleep that are approximately 45 minutes long. They first go into a deep sleep and then into R.E.M., a lighter sleep featuring dreams, and, finally, come to consciousness. These cycles are barely noticeable to most adults (unless a vivid dream wakes us). Usually, we just turn over and send ourselves back to sleep without realising we've woken.

Some infants do pretty much the same thing. You might hear them make grumpy little noises – which I call 'phantom baby' sounds. And as long as no one disturbs them, they're off to dreamland again.

Other infants coming out of R.E.M. sleep aren't able to send themselves back to sleep as easily. Often, it's because their parents rush in too quickly from the moment they're born and they never have an opportunity to learn how to shift gears going in and out of these natural sleep cycles.

The Yellow Brick Road to Dreamland

Sleep is a learned process that is initiated and reinforced by parents. Hence, they have to teach their babies how to get to sleep. And this is what the road to sensible sleep entails.

Pave the way for sleep

Because babies thrive on predictability and learn from repetition, we must always do and say the same things before naps or bedtime, so that in their baby minds they think, 'Oh, this means I'm going to sleep.'

Do the same rituals in the same order. Always check to see if she needs a change of nappy, as you want her to be comfortable. Go to the blinds or curtains and draw them shut.

Stress the benefits of rest in setting the mood. Don't present sleep as a punishment or struggle. If a child has been told, 'You're going for a nap' or 'You have to rest now,' in a tone that really says, 'You're banished to Siberia,' he or she grows up to become someone who thinks that naps are bad or that sleep means missing out on the fun.

Sleepytime signs

Like us, babies yawn when they start to get tired. The reason humans yawn is that as the body becomes fatigued, it doesn't work as efficiently; the normal supply of oxygen brought in by the lungs, heart and blood system diminishes a bit. Yawning is the body's way of gulping down extra oxygen. I tell parents to try to act on their baby's first yawn – if not the first, at least by the third. If you miss the signs (see below), certain types of infants, such as Touchy babies, quickly go into a meltdown. As infants get older, their changing bodies find new ways to tell you they're ready for sleep.

- *When they gain control over their heads*. As they become sleepier, they turn their face away from objects or people, as if trying to shut out the world. If carried, they bury their face into your chest. They make involuntary movements, flailing their arms and legs.

- *When they gain control of their limbs*. Tired babies may rub their eyes, pull at their ears, or scratch at their faces.

- *When they begin to gain mobility*. Babies who are getting tired become visibly less co-ordinated and lose interest in toys. If held, they'll arch their backs and lean backwards. In their cots, they can inch their way into a corner and may wedge their heads there. Or they'll roll one way and get stuck because they can't roll back.

• **When they can crawl and/or walk.** When older babies are tired, they lose their coordination. If trying to pull themselves up, they'll fall; if walking, they'll stumble or bump into things. They have full control of their own bodies, so they'll often cling to the adult who is trying to put them down. They can stand up in their cots but often don't know how to get back down – unless they fall, which frequently happens.

Wind down as you near the destination

Before bedtime, allow your baby time to wind down with a bath and, if she's three months or older, a massage will help prepare her for sleep (see page 23). Even at naptime, I always play a soothing lullaby. For about five minutes, I sit in a rocking chair or on the floor to give baby an extra snuggle. You also can tell her a story if you like, or just whisper sweet nothings into her ear. The purpose of this, however, is to calm your baby, not to make her fall asleep. Therefore, I stop the cuddle if I see the seven-mile stare – Stage 2 – or if her eyes are starting to close, which means she's already starting Stage 3. (It's never too early to begin bedtime stories, but I don't generally introduce books until around six months, when babies are better able to focus and sit up.)

> Don't invite guests to your house when you're putting your baby to bed.

Park her in her cot before she reaches dreamland

Many people think that you can't put a baby into her crib until she's fast asleep. That's simply wrong. Putting her down at the beginning of Stage 3 is the best way to help your baby develop the skills she needs to go to sleep on her own. There's another reason, too: babies who wake up somewhere different from where they fell asleep can end up not feeling comfortable or safe in their cot.

Some babies will naturally quieten themselves. But if she cries, a gentle, rhythmic pat on the back will give her the assurance that she's not alone. But remember to stop patting when she stops fussing – if you continue longer than she needs you to, she will begin to associate patting with going to sleep and, worse, begin to need it to get to sleep.

I usually suggest putting a baby down on her back. However, you can also put her to sleep on her side by wedging her with two rolled-up towels or special wedge-shaped cushions that can be purchased at most pharmacies. If she sleeps on her side, for her comfort, make sure it's not always the same side.

Dummies to aid sleep

I like to use a dummy during the first three months – the period when we're first establishing routines. This saves Mum from becoming a human dummy. At the same time, I always caution limited use so that the dummy doesn't turn into a prop. When used correctly, babies will suck ferociously for about six or seven minutes, then start to slow down a bit; eventually, they'll spit the dummy out. That's because they have expelled the sucking energy they needed to release and are on the way to dreamland. The important thing to remember is to take the dummy away after your baby has finished sucking and only reintroduce it if you have a similar situation another day.

Bear in mind that it takes 20 minutes for your baby to actually fall asleep, so don't ever try to rush things. If you do, she will get fussy and you will disrupt her natural three-stage process. For example, if she is disturbed during Stage 3 – say, by a loud bang, a dog barking or a door slamming – it will move her towards waking, not sleeping, and you will have to start all over again. It's no different from when an adult is drifting off and a telephone rings, jarring the silence. If the person gets annoyed or over-stimulated, it's sometimes hard to fall back to sleep. It's the same with your baby. If this happens, naturally she will fuss, the cycle must start again, and it just might take another 20 minutes for her to drift off.

When You Miss the Window

First, I'm going to tell you what *not* to do in this situation: never bounce or jiggle. Never walk or rock him too wildly. Remember that he is already over-stimulated. He's crying because he's already had enough, and crying is his way of blocking out sound and light.

Most sleep problems occur because one of the following happens before bedtime. The baby is:

- nursed

- walked around

- rocked or jiggled

- allowed to fall asleep on an adult's chest

- asleep, and the parents rush in at the first little whimper. (She might have fallen back to sleep on her own without their well-meaning interference. But she then becomes accustomed to being rescued.)

To avoid such a scenario, here's what you can do to help calm your baby and block out the outside world.

Swaddle

Fresh from a foetal position, infants are not used to wide-open spaces. Plus, they don't know that their arms and legs belong to them. When they're over-tired, you need to immobilise them, because seeing their appendages flail about both scares the living daylights out of them – they think someone's doing something to them – and the experience heaps more stimulation on to their already overloaded senses.

To swaddle properly, fold the corner of a square receiving blanket into a triangle. Lay your baby on top, positioning the fold level with his neck. Place one of his arms across his chest at a 45-degree angle and bring one corner of the blanket snugly across his body. Do the same with the other side.

I suggest swaddling for the first six weeks, but after the seventh week, when baby is first trying to get his hands to his mouth, help him out by bending his arms and leaving his hands exposed and close to his face.

Reassure

Let him know you're there to help him. Pat his back steadily and at an even pace, mimicking a heartbeat. You also can add a sound (sh… sh… sh… sh…) which simulates the rhythmic whooshing baby heard in the womb. Keep your voice low and soothing, and whisper into his ear, 'It's okay,' or 'You're only going to sleep.' As you put him down into his cot, if you've been patting, continue to pat. If you've been vocalising a reassuring sound, keep doing it. That makes for a smoother transition.

Block out visual stimulation

Visual stimulation – light, moving objects – assaults a tired baby, especially a Touchy one. This is why we darken the room before putting baby into bed, but for some, that's not enough. If your baby is lying down, place your hand over, not on, his eyes to block out the visuals. If you're holding him, stand still in a dimmed area or, if he's really agitated, in a totally dark closet.

Don't cave in

When a baby is over-tired, it's very hard on the parents. It takes tremendous patience and resolve, especially if the baby has already slipped into a bad habit. Their baby is screaming; they keep patting; the cries get louder. Over-stimulated babies tend to cry and cry until their high-pitched 'I'm exhausted!' wails reach a crescendo. Then they'll stop for a moment, and start all over again. Usually, there are three such crescendos before a baby finally calms down.

INDEPENDENCE IS NOT NEGLECT!

I never leave a screaming baby. On the contrary, I consider myself that baby's voice. If I don't help him, who will translate his needs? At the same time, I don't advocate holding or comforting a baby once you have met his need. The minute he's calm, put him down. Thus, you give him the gift of independence.

Sleeping Through the Night

Let's start this discussion by reminding you that your baby's 'day' is 24 hours long. She doesn't know the difference between day and night, so the idea of sleeping through the night means nothing to her. It's something you want (and need) her to do. It's not a natural occurrence; you will train her to do it, teach her that there's a difference between day and night. Here are some reminders I give parents.

Employ the robbing-Peter-to-pay-Paul principle

There is no doubt that keeping your baby on an E.A.S.Y. routine helps speed his sleeping through the night, because it's a structured yet flexible routine. During the day, never let a baby sleep more than a feed cycle – in other words, no longer than three hours – because otherwise it will rob his night-time sleep hours. I guarantee that any baby who has had six hours of uninterrupted sleep during the day will not sleep more than three at night. So if you find your baby doing this, you can be sure that his 'day' has now become your night. The only way to switch him round is by waking him, thereby robbing Peter of the hours your baby is using up by sleeping during the day, in order to pay Paul – adding those hours to the night-time sleep.

Tank them up

This might seem a rather crude expression, but one of the ways we get babies to sleep through the night is by filling their tummies. To that end, when an infant is six weeks old, I suggest two practices: cluster feeding – that is, feed her every two hours before bedtime – and giving what I call a 'dream feed' right before you retire for bed. For example, you give her the breast (or a bottle) at six and eight in the evening, and the dream feed at 10.30 or 11. With dream feeding, literally nurse or bottle-feed her in her sleep. In other words, you pick your baby up, gently place the bottle or breast on her lower lip, and allow her to eat, taking care not to wake her. When she's finished, you don't even burp her; just put her down. Infants are usually so relaxed at these feeds, they don't gulp air. You don't talk; you don't change her unless she's soaked through or soiled. With both these 'tanking-up' techniques, most babies can sleep through that middle-of-the-night feed, because they have enough calories to keep them going for five or six hours.

Use a dummy

> Have Dad take over the dream feed. Most men are usually home at the time, and the majority love doing it.

If it isn't allowed to become a prop, a dummy can be very helpful in weaning a baby off the night-time feed. If a baby weighs 4.5kg (10lb) and he's consuming at least 875–1000ml (30–35oz) of food during his daytime feeds or is getting between six and eight breastfeeds (four or five during the day; two or three clustered at night), he doesn't need an additional night feed for nourishment. If he's still waking, he's using the opportunity for oral stimulation. This is where prudent use of a dummy can pay off. If it normally takes your baby 20 minutes to feed at night, when he wakes up crying for the breast or bottle, and yet he only feeds for five minutes or takes barely an ounce, give him a dummy instead. The first night, he'll probably stay up the entire 20 minutes with the dummy in his mouth before falling back to sleep. The next night, it may cut back to 10 minutes. The third night, he might fidget in his sleep at the time he'd normally get up for the feed.

If he wakes, give him the dummy. In other words, you're substituting the oral stimulation of the dummy for the bottle or breast. Eventually, he won't wake up for it.

Don't rush in
At their best, babies often sleep fitfully (see 'Baby Sleep' page 98). That's why it's not wise to respond to every little noise you hear. In fact, I often tell parents to get rid of those monitors that exaggerate every coo and cry. They turn parents into alarmists and worrywarts! As I've repeated throughout this chapter, one must walk a fine line between responding and rescuing. A baby whose parents respond becomes a secure child who's not afraid to venture forth. A baby whose parents continually rescue begins to doubt his own capabilities and never develops the strength and skills he needs to explore his world or to feel comfortable in it.

Normal Sleep Disturbances

Normally good sleepers go through periods of restlessness and even have problems getting to sleep. Here are some of those times.

When solid food is introduced
Babies may wake up with wind once they begin ingesting solid food. Check with your health visitor or clinic to see what foods to introduce and when. Ask which foods could possibly cause wind or allergies. Keep a careful record of every food you've introduced so that if problems occur, your doctor can study your child's food history.

When they start moving about

Babies who have just learned how to control their movements often get a tingling in their limbs and joints. They're not used to movement. Sometimes, once they're able to wiggle about, they can get themselves into positions they can't get out of, and this, too, can disturb their sleep. They also may wake up confused, because they're in a different position. Just go in and reassure the baby with a rhythmic whisper: 'Sh... sh... sh... sh... you're okay.'

When they go through a growth spurt

During a growth spurt, babies sometimes wake up hungry. Feed your baby that night, but the next day give her more food during the day. The growth spurt may last for two days, but upping your baby's calories usually ends the sleep disturbance.

When they're teething

If it's teething and not some other problem, babies drool, their gums are red and swollen, and sometimes they have a low-grade fever. One of my favourite home remedies is to wet one corner of a washcloth, stick it in the freezer, and, when it's frozen solid, give it to Baby to suck on. I personally don't like shop-bought items that you freeze, because I don't know what kind of liquid is inside. Farley's Rusks – hard teething biscuits that melt down to nothing – are fantastic, safe and can be found in most shops. Bonjela also seems to be popular for helping with the pain.

When they have a dirty nappy

One mum I know calls them 'power poos' – and most infants wake up when they happen. Sometimes it even scares them. Change the nappy in dim light, to prevent your baby from getting revved up. Reassure her, and put her back to sleep.

What They Need/What You Can Expect		
Age/Milestones	Sleep Needed per Day	Typical Patterns
Newborn: doesn't have control over anything except his eyes	16–20 hours	Nap 1 hour in every 3; sleep 5–6 hours at night
1–3 months: More alert and aware of their surroundings; able to move head	15–18 hours, until 18 months of age	Three naps, 1½ hours each; 8 hours at night
4–6 months: Gaining mobility		Two naps, 2–3 hours each; 10–12 hours at night
6–8 months: More mobility; able to sit and crawl		Two naps, 1–2 hours each; 12 hours at night
8–18 months: Always in motion		Two naps, 1–2 hours each, or one big nap, 3 hours long; 12 hours at night

Whenever your baby wakes in the middle of the night, for whatever reason, never be too playful or friendly. Be loving, take care of the problem, but be careful not to give your baby the wrong idea. Otherwise, she might wake up the next night wanting to play.

CHAPTER EIGHT
The Y – You

One of the most important pieces of advice I give new parents during the first few days and weeks is this: you're a better parent than you think you are. Most don't realise that parenting is a learned art. Furthermore, all new mothers need time to heal. In addition to the physical trauma of childbirth, they're consumed with details they never thought about, more tired than they imagined they'd be, and overwhelmed by their emotions.

To me, the best rejuvenation of all is sleep. I send mums to bed between two and five every day. If you don't get enough rest, I guarantee that six weeks later you'll feel as if a bus has hit you. But don't let me be the one to say I told you so. For women, it helps to talk to good friends who have been through it, as well as your own mother if you have a good relationship with her – she can be a great support and remind you that this is a natural process.

It also helps to take things in small bites. Even if there's a mountain of laundry staring at you, you don't have to do it all. You'll have good days and not-so-good days; be prepared for both.

Recovery Reminders

The following reminders may seem elementary, my dear Watson, but you wouldn't believe how many mums don't keep them in mind.

- ***Eat***. Consume a balanced diet, at least 1,500 calories a day, 500 extra if you're breastfeeding. Don't watch your weight. Have food in the freezer or take-away menus on hand.

- ***Sleep***. Take a nap every afternoon at least, more often if you can. Give Dad a turn.

- ***Exercise***. Don't use equipment or train for at least six weeks; take long walks instead.

- ***Find a few moments for yourself***. Ask your spouse, a relative, or a friend to take over so that you can truly be 'off duty'.

- ***Don't make promises you can't keep***. Let others know you won't be available for at least a month or two. If you've already overbooked yourself, beg off: 'I'm sorry. I underestimated what having a baby would mean.'

- ***Prioritise***. Cross non-essentials off the list.

- ***Plan***. Line up baby-sitters; plan menus; make lists so that you shop only once a week. To resume pre-baby activities, like a weekly book club, co-ordinate with your spouse, a relative or a good friend.

- ***Know your own limitations***. When you're tired, lie down; when you're hungry, eat; and when you're irritable, leave the room!

- ***Ask for help***. No one can do this on her own.

- ***Spend time with your partner or a good friend***. Don't centre every minute around your newborn. All-baby-all-the-time is unrealistic.

- ***Pamper yourself***. As regularly as you can, have a massage (from someone familiar with postpartum bodies), a facial, a manicure and/or a pedicure.

The Many Moods of Mum

The first six weeks are a roller-coaster ride of emotions, and the only thing we can do is strap ourselves in and prepare for the ride. Remember: they're mood swings, which is why, within the course of a day, certainly a week, you might feel as if you're inhabited by a variety of personalities whose voices resonate inside you.

'This is pretty easy'
At these moments, you feel like the quintessential natural mother – you can figure it all out pretty quickly and easily. You trust your own judgement, feel confident, and aren't particularly susceptible to parenting trends. You can also laugh at yourself and know that motherhood isn't something you're going to do perfectly all the time. You're not afraid to ask questions, and when you do, you easily retain the answers or can adapt them to suit your own situation. You feel balanced.

'Am I doing this right?'
These are the anxiety-ridden moments when you feel inept and pessimistic. You may feel skittish about handling the baby, fearing that you might break her. The slightest glitch can upset you – in fact, you may even worry about events that haven't occurred. And at the extreme, perhaps when your hormones are raging most wildly, you imagine the worst.

'Oh, this is bad ... really, really bad'

At these moments, you moan and groan over your experience of childbirth and the ongoing saga of motherhood, and you're sure no one has ever felt this miserable – or else why would they have babies? It makes you feel better to tell everyone how painful the caesarean was, how the baby is keeping you up at night, how your husband is just not doing the things he promised he would. And when you're offered help, you're apt to play the martyr: 'It's all right. I'll handle it.'

'No problem – I'll just whip everything into shape'

Successful women who leave thriving careers to become mothers are most prone to moments like these. At such times, you think you can impose your management skills on to your baby, and you may be surprised, disappointed or angry when your infant doesn't cooperate. You're having a moment of denial, believing that life with baby will continue to be just as it was before he arrived.

'But the book says ...'

During moments of confusion and doubt, you read everything you can get your hands on and then try to apply it to your baby. To deal with the chaos, you make endless lists and use chalkboards and organisers. While I applaud structure and order, it's not good to be inflexible, letting your routine rule you rather than guide you.

Baby Blues or Real Depression?

Let me reiterate: some negativity is normal. All in the course of a typical postpartum period, women get hot flushes, headaches and dizzy spells; they may become lethargic or weepy; they may have feelings of self-doubt and anxiety. What causes these baby blues? Levels of the hormones oestrogen and progesterone drop radically within hours of delivery, as do levels of endorphins, which have contributed to feelings of joy and comfort during pregnancy. This causes one's emotions to swing wildly. Clearly, the stress of new motherhood is also a factor. Moreover, if you're prone to PMS, it means that your hormones typically give you a wild ride, so you can probably expect one after childbirth, too.

> If your baby is crying, you're alone with him, and you feel like you can't deal with it, or, worse, you feel anger rising, put him in the cot and leave the room. A baby never died of crying. Take three deep breaths and then come back. If you're still agitated, phone a relative, a friend or a neighbour and ask for help.

Baby blue days usually come in waves, which is why I call the force that propels them your 'inner tsunami'. A wave can drown out your sanity and sense of well-being for an hour or for a day or two; it might continue on and off for three months to a year. Baby blue days can colour how you feel about everything, most of all your infant. Those voices in your head are likely to chime in with 'What have I let myself in for?' or 'I can't manage the [you fill in the blank – nappies/breastfeeding/getting up in the middle of the night].'

It is estimated that 10–15 per cent of new mothers have postpartum depression; one in a thousand suffers a complete break with reality, known as postpartum psychosis. Other than hormonal changes and the stress of new motherhood, scientists are still unclear about why some women sink into a severe clinical depression after childbirth. One documented risk factor is a history of chemical imbalance. One-third of women with a history of depression experience depression postpartum as well; half of those who suffer from it after their first delivery relapse after subsequent births.

Sadly, even some doctors aren't aware of the risk. As a result, women often have no idea what's happening to them when the depression hits – a problem that could be avoided with information and education.

If you suspect that you have postpartum depression, consult your regular doctor or a psychiatrist.

If your baby blue days seem to linger, or if one bad day runs painfully into the next without much respite, seek professional help immediately. There is no shame in depression; it's a biological condition. It doesn't mean that you're a bad mum – it means you have an illness, no different from 'flu. Consequently, and most importantly, you can get medical help as well as support from other women who've been through it.

Dad's Reaction

Fathers are often given short shrift during the postpartum period. However, it is important to remember that just as mums have many moods, I've noticed certain 'father feelings' that crop up when baby arrives.

'Let me do it'

Sometimes, especially in the first few weeks, Dad is a really hands-on kind of guy. He is totally involved from pregnancy through delivery and then is into the baby in a big way. He's open to learn and eager to hear that he's doing a good job. He has good natural instincts with his baby as well, and you can tell from his face that he just loves being with her.

'It's not my job'

This is the reaction we'd expect from what we once thought of as a 'traditional' father – a guy who prefers a hands-off approach. Sure, he loves his baby, but not when it comes to changing nappies or giving the baby a bath. In his view, that's a woman's job. He believes he has a bona fide excuse not to do the boring, dirty work of childcare. In time, especially as the baby becomes more interactive, he may soften. I guarantee that he won't come round, though, if you harp on what he doesn't do, or compare him to other fathers.

'Oh, no – something's wrong'

This guy is tense and stiff when he first holds the baby. He may have done all the childbirth and parenting classes with his wife, but he's still terrified about doing something wrong. When he gives a bath, he frets about scalding; after he puts the baby to sleep, he worries about SIDS (Sudden Infant Death Syndrome). And when it's all quiet on the home front, he starts to wonder if he can afford to send the kid to college. Successful experiences with his baby usually build Dad's confidence and help dissipate these feelings. Gentle encouragement and applause from Mum can help, too.

'Look at this baby!'

This father is proud beyond belief. Not only does he want everyone to see his trophy baby, he may also inflate his own involvement. You'll hear him tell visitors, 'I let my wife sleep in the middle of the night.' Meanwhile, his exasperated wife is rolling her eyes behind his back. If this is his second marriage, even if he was a hands-off dad the first time round, he's now the expert, frequently correcting his wife with a dismissive comment such as 'That's not how I did it.' Give him his due, Mum, especially if he seems to know what he's doing, but don't let him override your best instincts.

'What baby?'

As I mentioned earlier, some mums go into denial when the baby comes. Well, dads have their own version. Regardless of a man's initial reaction, most do change, although often in ways that don't please their wives. When mums ask me, 'How do I get him to participate more?' they're disappointed because there's no magical answer. What I've found is that men become interested in their own ways and in their own time. An eager beaver may become less involved, while an unlikely nurturer suddenly throws himself into childcare once his baby begins to smile, sit, walk or talk. And most fathers tend to do best with concrete jobs that they feel they can do well. The 'secret' here is one of the underlying themes of this book: respect. If a man feels that his needs and wants are acknowledged, it is more likely that he will respect yours. But in the beginning, you ought to expect a bit of juggling about as each of you struggles to find your footing.

What About Us?

When baby makes three, the relationship between partners changes as well. In many cases, the reality rarely matches the dream. But it's usually problems under the surface that make a couple's connection come undone.

He said / she said

In any two-parent partnership, each person has a different perspective. I often act like a UN translator, telling one what the other wants him or her to know.

Mum wants me to tell her partner:

- how much the delivery hurts

- how tired she is

- how overwhelming breastfeeding is

- how much breastfeeding hurts (to demonstrate, I once pinched a dad's nipples and said, 'Let me just hold on like this for 20 minutes')

- that she's crying or yelling because she's hormonal, not because of him

- that she can't explain why she's crying

Dad wants me to tell his partner:

- to stop criticising everything he does

- that the baby isn't made from china and won't break

- that he's doing his best

- that it hurts him when she dismisses his ideas about the baby

- that he's feeling more pressure now to provide for his new family

- that he's depressed and overwhelmed, too

Beginners' jitters

Mum feels overburdened. Dad doesn't quite know what to do to help. I like to give specific jobs to Dad – shopping, bath, the dream feed – that make him feel part of the process. After all, Mum needs every bit of help she can get. I urge men to be their wife's ears and her memory. Besides the fact that there's so much new information to absorb, many women suffer from postpartum amnesia, a temporary condition that nevertheless drives them absolutely crazy. Or there may be a special need that a father can fulfil.

Gender differences

Whatever conflict occurs between Mum and Dad in those first few weeks, I inevitably remind them that they're in this together, although they may see their situation from very different points of view. Couples do best when they learn not only to translate but also not to take it personally when one sees things differently from the other. They should find strength in their dissimilarities, because then they have a broader repertoire to draw from.

Lifestyle shifts

With some couples, the major stumbling block is learning how to change the way they make plans. They may have lots of relatives who help out, or paid nannies, but they're not good at scheduling their time to include a dependent third party – because they've never had to.

Calling All Partners!

A few words of wisdom to the one who hasn't given birth and isn't spending all day at home with the new baby:

DO

- take a week or more off work; if you can't afford to, save money to get someone in to do the housework

- listen without having a solution

- offer support lovingly and without comment

- take no for an answer when she says she doesn't want your help

- shop, clean, do laundry and vacuum without her having to ask

- recognise that she has a good reason when she says, 'I don't feel like myself'

DON'T

- try to 'fix' her emotional or physical problems – ride them out

- be a cheerleader or patronise her – for example, by patting her behind and saying 'good job', as if she's a dog

- walk into your own kitchen and wonder aloud where something is kept

- stand over her and criticise

- call home from the shop if they're out of smoked turkey to ask, 'What should I get instead?' – figure it out yourself

Couple Care 101

DO

- schedule time together – perhaps a walk, date night or trip to the pub

- plan a childless vacation, even if you can't actually take one for a while

- hide surprise messages for your partner

- give an unexpected present

- send a love letter to the office, telling her/him all that you adore and appreciate

- always be kind and respectful to one another

Sex and the Suddenly Stressed-out Spouse

Talk about your 'he said / she said' issues. Sex is the number one topic on every father's to-do list, and usually at the bottom of most mums'. Indeed, the first question he asks when she comes home from the gynaecologist after her postpartum check-up is: 'Did he say we could have sex?'

Sex after childbirth does change. We do parents an injustice when we don't warn them. Men who want sex straight away often don't realise the extent to which a woman's body transforms with childbirth. Her breasts are sore, her vagina has been stretched, her labia have been extended, lower levels of hormones can make her dry. Breastfeeding can complicate the picture further. If a woman formerly liked to have her nipples stimulated, she may find it painful now, or repugnant – her breasts suddenly belong to her baby.

So what does a couple do? There's no instant solution here, but some of these suggestions usually take the pressure off both parties.

Talk about it openly
Rather than allowing emotions to bubble under the surface, admit how you really feel.

Look at your sex life before you became parents
If your sex life wasn't that good before the baby, it's certainly not going to improve afterwards. Couples need to have realistic expectations about their sex lives. It stands to reason that the issue of post-baby sex affects a couple more if they've been bonking three nights a week and suddenly stop than if they did it once a week or once a month.

Keep your priorities straight
Decide together what's important to you now, and allow for re-evaluation in a few months. If you both decide that lovemaking is important, make time and space for it. Plan a date night once a week.

Get a baby-sitter and get out of the house. If your partner is not physically and emotionally ready, back off. Pressure is not an aphrodisiac.

Lower your expectations

Sex is intimate, but not all intimacy is sex. If you're not ready for lovemaking, find other ways to be intimate. For example, go to a concert together and hold hands. Or consider a 'make-out session' where you do nothing but kiss for an hour. I always admonish men to be patient. Women need time. Also, a man should not take a woman's reluctance personally. In fact, I suggest that guys try to imagine what it must be like to carry and then expel a little being. I mean, how soon afterwards would they want sex under those conditions?

> Mum, when you and Dad take an evening out, don't talk about the baby. You've physically left your little bundle of joy at home, where she should be. Unless you want subconscious resentment to build on Dad's part, leave her home emotionally as well.

Sex After Childbirth

How women feel

- *Exhausted*: 'Sex just feels like one more chore.'

- *Overwrought*: 'Everyone seems to be taking from me.'

- *Guilty*: They're depriving their child or their spouse.

- *Ashamed*: 'If the baby is in the next room, I feel like I'm sneaking.'

- *Uninterested*: 'It's the last thing on my mind.'

- *Self-conscious*: They feel fat and 'weird' about their breasts.

- *Wary*: 'If he kisses me on the cheek, says "I love you", or puts an arm around my waist, it feels like an expectation – the first stage of lovemaking.'

How men feel

- *Frustrated*: 'How long do we have to wait?'

- *Rejected*: 'Why doesn't she want me?'

- *Jealous*: 'She cares more about the baby than me.'

- *Resentful*: 'The baby takes all her time.'

- *Angry*: 'Isn't she ever going to be back to normal?'

- *Confused*: 'Is it okay to ask her to have sex?'

- *Duped*: 'She said if the doctor said it's okay, we would have sex, but it has been weeks since then.'

Neighbours, Friends and Relatives: Creating a Circle of Support

No matter what your situation, it's important to try to create your own circle of support, one person if not several, who will cheer you on and insist that you take it easy.

Assess your relationships with various family members. Are you close to your own mum? If so, there's no one who knows you better. She loves her new grandchild, so she has the baby's safety at heart. She has experience, too. When I work in a household with a cooperative grandma or grandpa, it's wonderful. I give everyone a to-do list, anything from vacuuming to sticking stamps on envelopes – things Mum shouldn't even be thinking about at this point.

Maintaining your circle of support

Here's how to make the most of unpaid help:

- Don't expect people to read your mind – ask for help.

- Especially in the first six weeks, ask people to shop, cook, bring in food, clean, do laundry – so that you have time to be with and get to know your baby.

- Be realistic. Ask of people only what they can actually do – don't send a forgetful dad to the grocery shop without a list; don't ask your mum to baby-sit at the time when you know she has a regular tennis game.

- Write down your baby's schedule so that others understand what the day is like and can work around it.

- Apologise when you snap … because you will!

New mums often ask me how to field unsolicited advice, especially when relationships are strained to begin with. I advise them to keep advice in perspective. This is a sensitive time. You're just getting your footing. If someone suggests a technique or practice that's different from what you're doing, even if the advice is meant to help, it can feel like criticism. So before you immediately conclude that you're under fire, consider the source. Chances are the person is genuinely trying to be helpful and may have some good pointers to share. Take it all in and then decide what's right for you.

Respond to unsolicited advice by saying, 'Wow, that's really interesting – it sounds like it really worked for your family,' even though in your head you may be saying, 'I'm going to do it my way.'

Work: Going Back Without Guilt

Whether a woman leaves a high-powered career, a cosy office job, a volunteer position, or even a beloved hobby behind because she wants to have a baby, there usually comes a time – for some women a month after delivery, for others several years later – when the question 'What about me?' begins to niggle. Of course, some women already have a game plan in place during pregnancy about when they'll return to work or resume a particular project. Others play it by ear. Either way, they deal with the same two questions: 'How will I do this without feeling guilty?' and 'Who will care for the baby?' At least in my mind, the first question is a simpler one, so let's deal with that straight away.

Guilt is the curse of motherhood. I don't know when, where or why guilt was invented, but it's an epidemic these days. Maybe it's part of perfectionism, but the way I see it, you're damned if you do, damned if you don't. Some women in my classes feel utterly inadequate because they're 'just mums' or 'just housewives'. Working mums, though, whether going off to impressive careers or to menial jobs that simply pay the bills, feel just as bad about themselves, but for different reasons.

Working doesn't make women bad mothers. It makes them women who are empowered enough to say, 'This is how it's going to be.'

Clearly, some women have no financial choice but to work. Others work for their own self-satisfaction. Whether or not pay is involved, though, the point is that these women are doing things that feed their grown-up selves. And they needn't apologise, any more than the mother who is contentedly managing her home.

There's nothing wrong with wanting at the very least to be able to answer phone calls, to have lunch with friends, to feel like you're something other than a mother.

If you want or need to work 12 hours a day, figure out ways to make your time at home more meaningful. For example, don't pick up the phone when you are with your kids. Take it off the hook or let the answering machine field all calls. Don't work on weekends. And when you're at home, keep

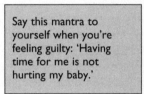

Say this mantra to yourself when you're feeling guilty: 'Having time for me is not hurting my baby.'

your mind at home rather than in the office. Even babies sense when you're not really there.

When you come home from work, you should always change out of your work clothes, even if you're in an office all day. Clothing retains smells of the outside that can upset baby's delicate senses (and you won't have to worry about getting non-work clothes messed up).

Who's Going to Look After the Baby?

It's a difficult matter at best – and very stressful. Finding the right childcare is an arduous process. But your child is your most precious –

and irreplaceable – possession; hiring someone to care for her should be a top priority.

Give yourself at least two months, ideally three, to conduct a search. If, for example, you plan to go back to work when your baby is six or eight weeks old, that means you have to start when you're pregnant. Put all your insight and energy into the search. Below are some other points you need to consider.

Hiring a child care provider

The first step, obviously, is to assess your own situation. The more details you focus on, before you even begin your search, the better equipped you'll be to conduct the interviews. This applies whether you are hiring a nanny, a childminder or placing your child in a nursery.

If you're thinking of hiring a nanny, for example, write a job description of everything you want her to do. That way, you'll be clear on what you want, and when you're talking to candidates, you can share every detail – not only duties related to the baby and to your household, but also salary, days off, restrictions, holidays, bonuses and overtime.

There are a good many reputable agencies, but they usually charge fees equal to a percentage of the nanny's annual salary. The better agencies carefully screen their nannies and can save you the time it takes to eliminate undesirable applicants. However, some fly-by-night operations do more harm than good. They don't check references carefully; some even lie about a person's qualifications and history. The best way to find a good agency is word of mouth. Ask friends about their experiences. If no one you know has used an agency, look in parenting magazines or the Yellow Pages. Ask them how many nannies they place each year – a good-sized agency will place a large number each year. Ask about their fee and find out what it includes – among other points, how extensive are background checks? What happens if the nanny doesn't work out? Are there any guarantees? If they don't find someone to your satisfaction, you shouldn't have to pay a fee.

Pay close attention during the interview. Find out what the nanny is looking for in a job. Does it match your description? If not, discuss the differences. What kind of training has she had? Ask her to talk about previous jobs and why she left them. Beyond baby care, does this woman have the skills that you require, such as driving, and personal attributes that will make for a good working relationship? Ask about her health (particularly if you have animals, as allergies might be an issue). Is she the right person for you? Chemistry is important.

Nanny red flags

- She's had many recent positions. Perhaps she works only in short stints, or she also could have problems getting on with employers. In contrast, when someone has held only one or two long-term positions in three years, it usually indicates competence and commitment.

- She's had no recent positions. That might be because she's been ill or is unemployable.

- She talks badly about other mums. One I interviewed went on and on about how the woman at her last job was a bad mum because she worked too late every night. Why she hadn't discussed that with her employer is beyond me.

- She has toddlers of her own. Her kids' germs will come to work with her, or she might have emergencies of her own, leaving you in the lurch.

- She needs a work permit. This may not be an insurmountable problem if you're willing to help. But if you don't factor this in, your beloved nanny could risk deportation.

- Your gut feeling is bad. Trust yourself. Don't hire anyone you don't feel good about.

Do your own background check. Ask each prospect to supply at least four references from former employers as well as a driver's licence, which will tell you something about how responsible she is. Call every one of her references, but also visit at least two to meet them in person. If someone offers a glowing testimonial, it's best to meet that person, too.

Do an at-home visit. Once you've narrowed your search, arrange to meet on her turf. Meet her children, if possible. Although it's not always an indication of how she'll interact with your baby, especially if her children are older, you'll at least get a sense of her warmth and her standards of cleanliness and care.

Bear in mind your own responsibilities. This is a partnership of sorts – you're not hiring a slave. The job description works both ways, so don't pile on extra responsibilities. If you didn't hire her to do housework, for example, you shouldn't expect her to do it once she's on the job. Give her all the resources she needs to do her job well – instructions, pocket money, everyday telephone numbers, phone numbers to be used in case of emergency. Remember, too, that she has personal needs of her own – for days off and time with her own family and friends.

Reassess regularly

Whatever childcare you opt for, reassess the situation on a regular basis and correct mistakes immediately. The best way to sustain a good relationship with anyone is through honest communication, and with childcare staff, it's vital. Ask anyone looking after your child to keep what I call a daily 'nannilog' (see below), so you will know what has gone on in your absence. Also, if your baby behaves unusually at night or has some sort of allergic reaction, you'll then be in a better position to assess why. Be candid and direct whenever you make suggestions or ask a nanny, childminder or nursery employee to do something differently. Have these conversations in private, and be sensitive in your delivery.

Keeping a 'nannilog'

Ask your child care provider to keep a simple daily record of what happens when you're not there. Below is a sample. Tailor your own 'nannilog' to suit your circumstances. It should be detailed but brief, so that it doesn't take your child provider much time to complete.

Unspoken fears about having someone else take care of your baby can colour your opinion of your child provider's conduct. Jealousy is a normal and common reaction. My advice is to talk about your feelings with your partner or a good friend. Know that there's no shame in having them; almost all mothers have been there. Just remember that you're the mum, and there's no substitute for that.

Foods

Bottles at _____ _____ _____ _____
New food introduced today: _____
Baby's reaction: ❑ Gas   ❑ Hiccups   ❑ Vomiting   ❑ Diarrhoea
Details:_____

Activities

Indoors: ❑ Gymini for _____ minutes   ❑ Playpen
Other: _____

Outdoors: ❑ Walk to park   ❑ Class   ❑ Pool
Other: _____

Milestones

❑ Smiled ❑ Lifted head ❑ Rolled over ❑ Sat up ❑ Stood up ❑ Took first step
Other: _____

Appointments

Doctor _____
Play dates_____

Extraordinary Occurrences

Accidents_____
Temper tantrum_____
Anything else out of the ordinary_____

CHAPTER NINE
The ABC Cure for Accidental Parenting

Clearly, no couple intends for their family life to turn upside down – hence I use the term 'accidental parenting'. I get sometimes as many as five to 10 calls a week from parents who didn't start as they meant to go on. They make comments such as 'He won't let me put him down' or 'She only eats for 10 minutes at a time', as if the baby is deliberately resisting what's best. What really has happened is that the parents unintentionally reinforced a negative behaviour.

My purpose in this chapter is not to make you feel bad but to teach you how to turn back the clock and undo the unwanted consequences of accidental parenting. And believe me, if your baby does something that upsets your household, disrupts your sleep, or prevents you from having a normal, everyday life, there is always something that you can do about it. However, we must start with these three basic premises:

1. *Your baby isn't being wilful or spiteful.* Parents are often unaware of the impact they have on their children, and that, for better or for worse, they shape their babies' expectations.
2. *You can 'untrain' your baby.* By analysing your own behaviour – what you do to encourage your baby – you'll be able to figure out how to change whatever bad habits you've unwittingly encouraged.
3. *Changing habits takes time.* If your baby is under three months old,

it usually takes three days, or even less. But if your baby is older and a particular pattern has persisted, you will have to make changes in steps. It will take more time – usually each step takes three days – and require a fair amount of patience on your part to 'fade out' whatever behaviour it is you're trying to change.

The ABC of Changing Bad Habits

I've devised a strategy to enable parents to analyse their part in the problem and, in doing so, help them figure out how they can change a difficult pattern. It's a simple ABC technique:

- *'A' stands for the antecedent*: what came first. What were you doing at the time? What did you do for your baby – or not do? What else was going on in his environment?

- *'B' stands for the behaviour*: your baby's part in what's happening. Is she crying? Does she look and sound angry? Scared? Hungry? Is what she's doing something that she usually does?

- *'C' stands for the consequence*: what kind of pattern has been established as a result of A and B. Accidental parents, unaware of how they may be reinforcing a pattern, keep doing what they always did – for example, rocking the baby to sleep or thrusting a breast in his mouth. The action may stop the present behaviour for a few minutes, but it will strengthen the habit in the long run. The key to changing the consequence, therefore, is to do something different – introduce a new behaviour in order to allow the old one to disappear.

By using my ABC strategy, you encourage the old behaviour to fade out. In three-day increments, you withdraw whatever it was you once did – fade out the old – in favour of something that builds your child's independence and resourcefulness. I call it the 'three-day magic' (although it's really just common sense). The older babies get, of course, the harder it will be to discourage the old behaviour. In fact, most of my calls for help come from parents with babies five months or older.

Sleep problems

Whether it's a baby who doesn't sleep through the night (after three months) or one who has trouble falling asleep independently, it's always a matter of, first, getting her used to her own bed, and then teaching her to sleep in it without being soothed. In worst-case scenarios, typically when accidental parenting has gone on for several months, the baby may be afraid of her own bed. Sometimes it's a case of her being used to your holding or rocking her. The *consequence* is that she never learned how to fall asleep on her own.

Feeding problems

When bad eating habits are the problem, the *antecedent* is usually some form of parents' misreading their baby's cues. No matter what the behaviour, the first thing I do is suggest a structured routine. With E.A.S.Y., there's less guesswork because parents know when babies are supposed to be hungry, and they can then look for other reasons for their infant's crankiness. But I also encourage parents to observe what's going on, to assess whether their baby really needs to eat, and if not, to then gradually fade out unnecessary extra feeds and to teach their child other ways of self-soothing. I may cut extra feeds shorter at first, allowing the baby to spend less time on the breast or take less bottle. I might switch to water, or use a dummy to make the transition complete. In the end, the baby won't even remember the old habit, which is why it looks like magic.

'He won't let me put him down'

This is another common problem, so what's the solution? Alter the *consequence* by changing what you do. Instead of holding him endlessly, pick him up when he starts to cry, but put him down as soon as he is calm. If he cries again, pick him up. When he quiets, lay him down again. And so on and so on. You might have to pick that baby up 20 or 30 times or more. In essence, you're saying, 'You're fine. I'm here. It's okay to be on your own.' I promise this won't go on for ever – unless you go back to your practice of comforting him past his need.

'But my baby has colic'

Here's where my three-day magic is really put to the test. Your baby wails and pulls his legs to his chest and seems to cry for hours at a time, and you think your baby has colic. However, colic has become a much-overused term, a catch-all word to describe almost any difficult situation. And many of those difficult situations can be made better.

I grant you, if your baby suffers from colic, it can be a nightmare – for the baby and for you. It is estimated that 20 per cent of babies suffer from some form of colic, and of those, 10 per cent are considered severe cases. In a colicky baby, the muscle tissue that surrounds the wee thing's gastrointestinal or genito-urinary tract begins to contract spasmodically. The symptoms usually start with fussing and then lead to prolonged bouts of crying, sometimes for hours on end. Typically, the attacks come at approximately the same time every day. Paediatricians sometimes use the 'rule of three' in diagnosing colic – three hours of crying per day, three days a week, for three weeks or more.

Colic often appears suddenly in the third or fourth week and seems to disappear just as mysteriously at around three months. (There's really no mystery. In most cases, the digestive system matures and the spasms abate. At that age, too, babies have greater control over their limbs and can find their own fingers to self-soothe.) However, in my experience, some of what is labelled colic may be a by-product of accidental parenting – a mum (or dad) desperate to calm a crying newborn slips into a pattern, the *antecedent*, of either rocking her infant to sleep or giving him breast or bottle for solace. This seems to 'cure' the child, at least for a bit. In the meantime, the baby begins to expect this kind of comforting whenever he's upset. By the time he's a few weeks old, the *consequence* is that nothing less will calm him, and everyone assumes it's colic.

Give yourself a break

In a roomful of mothers, even if none of the babies is crying, it's easy to recognise the mum with the colicky infant. She's the one who looks the most exhausted. She thinks it's her fault that somehow she ended up with a 'bad' baby. Nonsense. If your baby has true colic, it's a problem, to be sure, but you didn't cause it. And in order to ride it out, you need as much support as your baby does.

Instead of laying blame – which, sadly, some couples do – you and your partner need to relieve each other. With many babies, the crying comes like clockwork – say, from three to six every day. So take turns. If Mum is on duty one day, Dad should handle the next day.

If you're a single mum, try to enlist a grandparent, sibling or friend to stop by during the witching hour. And when relief comes, don't sit there listening to your baby cry. Get out of the house. Take yourself for a walk or a ride – do anything that gets you out of the environment.

Most importantly, remember this: although it feels as though your baby's colic will last for ever, I assure you that it will pass.

Tummyache techniques

Food management is the best way to avoid wind, but at some point your baby probably will have a tummyache. Here are the strategies I've found most effective:

- The best way to burp any baby, especially one with wind, is to rub upward on the left side (where her stomach is) using the heel of your palm. If after five minutes baby hasn't given you a burp, put her down. If she then starts to pant, squirm, roll her eyes, and make an expression that resembles a smile, she has wind. Pick her up, making sure her arms are over your shoulder and her legs straight down, and try burping her again.

- While your baby is lying on his back, pull his legs up and gently do a bicycling motion.

- Lay your baby across your forearm, facedown, and use your palm to put gentle pressure on her tummy.

- Make a cummerbund by folding a receiving blanket into a 12cm (5in) band and wrap it snugly around your baby's middle – but not tight enough to cut off her circulation (if she goes blue, it's too snug).

- To help your baby expel wind, hold him against you and pat his bottom. This gives him a focus point so that he knows where to push.

- Massage her tummy in a backward C motion (not a circle) so that you trace the colon – left to right, down, and then right to left.

Although paediatricians sometimes prescribe a mild antacid to relieve wind, nothing actually cures colic. But I do know that proper food management and the promotion of sensible sleep usually ease a baby's discomfort. Moreover, over-feeding and a lack of sleep can cause behaviour that looks like colic.

'Our baby won't give up the breast'

This is a complaint I often hear from fathers, especially if they're turned off by breastfeeding in the first place, or if their wives are continuing to nurse past the first year. It can lead to a very bad family situation if Mum doesn't realise that she is the reason baby stubbornly clings to her breast. My feeling is that when mothers prolong nursing, it's almost always for them, not for the baby. A woman often loves the role, the closeness and the secret knowledge that only she can calm the baby. Aside from finding breastfeeding peaceful or personally fulfilling, she might just relish the idea of her child being so dependent upon her.

Being a parent requires both introspection and balance. Many of the so-called problems I see arise because mums and dads don't realise how much of themselves they project on to their babies. It's always important to ask yourself, 'Am I doing this for my baby or for me?' I often see parents hold their babies when they no longer need to be held, or nursing long after their babies cease to need breast milk.

Remember, take it one baby step at a time:

1. observe and figure out a strategy
2. do each step slowly – you can't rush the process
3. solve one problem before moving on to the next
4. expect some regression since old habits die hard; you must commit yourself to the plan

Trouble-shooting Guide

The following is not meant to be an exhaustive list of every problem you might encounter, but these are the kinds of long-term difficulties I'm often asked to interpret and correct. If your baby has more than one, remember that you have to take one at a time. Ask yourself, 'What do I want to change?' and 'What do I want in its place?' And when trying to figure out what to do first, use your common sense – the solution is often more obvious than you think.

'My baby likes to be held all the time'

- *Likely antecedent*: You (or a baby nurse) probably liked to hold her in the beginning. Now she's used to it, and you're ready to get on with your life.

- *What you need to do*: When your baby needs comforting, pick her up and calm her, but put her down the minute she stops crying. Tell her, 'I'm right here – I didn't go anywhere.' Don't extend the length of time you hold her past her need for comfort.

'My baby seems to take almost an hour to feed'

- *Likely antecedent*: She may be using you as a human dummy. Are you on the phone when you feed her, or otherwise not paying attention to how she's eating?
- *What you need to do*: At first, a baby's sucking is usually ferocious and quick, and you'll hear her gulping down the 'quencher'. As she finally gets to the rich hind milk, she'll take long, harder strokes. But when she's pacifying, you'll see her bottom jaw going, but you won't feel the pulling. Tune in so that you know how your baby feeds. Don't let feeds go longer than 45 minutes.

'My baby is hungry every hour or hour and a half'

- *Likely antecedent*: You may be misreading her cues, interpreting every cry as hunger.
- *What you need to do*: Instead of giving her the bottle or breast, change her scene – she might be bored – or give her a dummy to satisfy her need to suck.

'My baby needs a bottle / the breast to go to sleep'

- *Likely antecedent*: You may have conditioned him to expect it by giving him the breast or a bottle before bedtime.
- *What you need to do*: Put your baby on E.A.S.Y. so that he doesn't associate sleep with breast or bottle. Also see Chapter 7, 'The S – Sleep', for hints about helping a baby learn how to sleep independently.

'My baby is five months old and doesn't sleep through the night'

- *Likely antecedent*: Your baby may have switched day for night. Think back to your pregnancy. If she kicked a lot at night and slept during the day, she came in with that biorhythm. Or you allowed her to take long daytime naps in her first few weeks, and now she's used to it.

- *What you need to do*: It's important to switch your baby around by waking her every three hours during the day. The first day she'll be lethargic, the second day more alert, and by the third you've changed her biological clock.

'My baby can't get himself to sleep without our rocking him'

- *Likely antecedent*: You may be missing his sleep cues and he's getting over-tired. Because you've probably rocked him to calm him, he hasn't learned to fall asleep on his own.

- *What you need to do*: Look for the first or second yawn. If you've been doing this for a while, he links rocking with sleep. As you phase out the rocking, you'll have to substitute other behaviour. Either stand still when you hold him or sit in a chair without rocking. Use your voice and patting instead of movement.

'My baby cries all day'

- *Likely antecedent*: If it's literally all day, it could be a matter of over-feeding, fatigue, and/or over-stimulation.

- *What you need to do*: Babies rarely cry that much, so it's best to consult your doctor. If it is colic, that surely isn't your doing; you'll have to ride it out. But if it's not colic, you may need to change your approach. In either case, putting a baby on E.A.S.Y. and promoting sensible sleep usually helps.

'My baby always wakes up cranky'

- *Likely antecedent*: Temperament aside, some babies are cranky when they wake up because they haven't had a proper amount of sleep. If you're getting your baby up when she's just shifting sleep gears, she may not be getting enough rest.

- *What you need to do*: Don't rush into her room the minute she makes a peep. Wait for a few moments to allow her to fall back to sleep on her own. Extend her naps during the day. Believe it or not, this will make her sleep better at night, because she won't be so over-tired.

Epilogue

Some Final Thoughts

I want to end this book with a very important reminder: have fun!

All the baby-whispering advice in the world is useless if you're not having a good time being a parent. Yes, I know it can be hard, especially in the earliest months, especially when you're exhausted. But you must always keep in mind what a special gift it is to be a parent.

Remember, too, that raising a child is a lifelong commitment – something you must take more seriously than any mission you've ever accomplished. You are responsible for helping to guide and shape another human being, and there is no greater, higher assignment.

When the going gets particularly rough (and I guarantee that, even with an Angel baby, at times it will), try not to lose perspective. Your child's babyhood is a wondrous age – scary, precious and all too fleeting. If you doubt for a moment that you'll someday look back with longing at this sweet, simple time, talk to parents of older kids who will tell you that taking care of a baby is but a tiny blip on the radar of your life – clear, sharp and sadly irretrievable.

My wish for you is to relish every moment, even the tough ones. My goal is to give you not merely information or skills, but something even more important: confidence in yourself and in your own ability to solve problems.

Yes, dear reader, you can empower yourself. Mum or Dad, Granny or Grandad – whoever has this book in hand – these secrets are no longer mine alone. Use them well, and enjoy the wonder of calming, connecting and communicating with your baby.

Index

☐ Secrets of the Baby Whisperer	9780091857028	£10.99
☐ Secrets of the Baby Whisperer for Toddlers	9780091884598	£10.99
☐ Tops Tips from the Baby Whisperer for Toddlers	9780091917432	£6.99

FREE POST AND PACKING
Overseas customers allow £2.00 per paperback.

ORDER:

By phone: 01624 677237

By post: Random House Books
c/o Bookpost
PO Box 29
Douglas
Isle of Man, IM99 1BQ

By fax: 01624 670923

By email: bookshop@enterprise.net

Cheques (payable to Bookpost) and credit cards accepted

Prices and availability subject to change without notice.
Allow 28 days for delivery.
When placing your order, please mention if you do not wish to receive
any additional information.

www.rbooks.co.uk